D0146323

Religion as Creative Insecurity

Religion as Creative Insecurity

Peter A. Bertocci

Borden Parker Bowne Professor of Philosophy

Boston University

GREENWOOD PRESS, PUBLISHERS
WESTPORT, CONNECTICUT

Library of Congress Cataloging in Publication Data

Bertocci, Peter Anthony.
    Religion as creative insecurity.

    Reprint of the ed. published by Association Press,
New York.
    Bibliography: p.
    1. Religion--Philosophy. 2. Security (Psychology)
I. Title.
BL51.B543 1973   201   73-1836
ISBN 0-8371-6803-1

Originally published in 1958 by Association Press, New York

Reprinted with the permission of Peter Bertocci

Reprinted by Greenwood Press,
a division of Williamhouse-Regency Inc.

First Greenwood Reprinting 1973
Second Greenwood Reprinting 1976

Library of Congress Catalog Card Numbe r73-1836

ISBN 0-8371-6803-1

Printed in the United States of America

To
Gaetano Bertocci
and
John Soldani

Acknowledgments

The paragraph in a manuscript an author best enjoys is the one in which he can acknowledge some of the debt he feels to friends who have shared directly and indirectly in his work. To my colleagues Richard M. Millard and John H. Lavely, and to my brother, Angelo, I am indebted for suggestions as they read earlier sections of what appears here. Without my wife and three sons I could not have had some of the experiences which give rise to this book. But I have in mind especially so many of my students who, in seeking higher education, have joined their parents in giving up what to others have been the "necessities" and "niceties" of life. They have shown a kind of heroism which makes teaching a constant discipline in humility. And I derive deep satisfaction from dedicating this book to my father and father-in-law who have exhibited in different ways the unobtrusive heroism of so many immigrants to America—a heroism almost impossible for their children to appreciate, but which must not be forgotten.

Contents

Foreword

Our age, someone has said, is an aspirin age. Perhaps we should now call it an "age of tranquilizers." We must reduce tensions, we are told on all sides, avoid conflicts, relax. One advertisement in a public bus urges us to take our worries to church and leave them there!

In this book I shall argue that this flight from insecurity is catastrophic to any kind of human growth. To flee from insecurity is to miss the whole point of being human. It is to miss, at any rate, the whole point of religion, and of the Christian faith in particular. Religion at its best is never a sedative for nerves. That a religion whose symbol is the Cross should be hailed as an antidote for insecurity testifies to the seductive power of the current yearning for security.

True, most of the time we live as if the purpose of life were to avoid suffering. But the problem of life is not, Shall we suffer?—as if anyone could be sensitively alive and avoid suffering in his own life, or suffering with others in their distress, for which he is sometimes to blame! The real problem of life is, For what shall we suffer? To this question I believe the Christian faith and mature living address themselves. Was it not Jesus who defined that creative insecurity which brings not "happiness" but blessedness? Peace, for him, was not a flight from insecurity. The peace he offered—"not as the

ix

world giveth"—was a peace in which he was able to "set his face toward Jerusalem" and be lifted up on a cross.

But the flight from insecurity and the search for peace of mind take on many subtle and sophisticated disguises. I shall here mention two, the cult of *scientism*, and the vogue of neo-orthodoxy.

So many persons who despise the sentimentality of "peace of mind" religion take their stand on the mighty rock of "scientific" dogma. They will not trust either soul or body to any conviction not inspired by the antiseptic ritual of a restricted Scientific Method. This method alone, they hold, reveals trustworthy laws to which we can conform our actions; for now, at last, we have Truth open to mathematical treatment and to public inspection by all who have eyes to see. The faith of this cult, which has often seemed to overrun both the physical and the social sciences, is in a Nature that will display its secret uniformities in response to the cultist's set-up experiments and "observations." It offers, to all who will carefully sterilize their intellectual instruments and discipline their emotions, a new faith in what man can do with man and with Nature.

But has not this cult of scientism lost the truly searching spirit of scientific explorers who faced the universe not simply to corral and harness it, but to understand it in its own terms? Nature spoke to them, and it was not a prepared speech! They did not simply manipulate Nature; they respected and loved it—and in a spirit of grateful and fresh wonder. They climbed dangerously and without despair, from precipice to precipice, following the contours of things instead of limiting the vistas to their convenient highways insured for safety. No, the cult of scientism has sold its birthright of creative insecurity for the specialized securities of the laboratory. Scientism, this *Ersatz* for science, "tranquilizes" its devotees with a false security by focusing vision upon a limited conquest rather than an incalculable adventure.

I should like to be able to say that contemporary theology, for all its "existentialist" stirring, had something really better to offer. Many theologians are inclined to lay the blame for the disastrous world-situation upon the overweening scientistic spirit and its supporting philosophy. They would agree that scientism offers an illusory security; but they do not attack the fetish of security itself. They have not really challenged peace-of-mind science and peace-of-mind religion at the center. They have substituted security for *security!* True security, they say, is not found through man's power to think, for even if man's ability to reason were greater than it is, man's unregenerate pride, his inordinate capacity to idolize himself and his achievements, would bar the way to God. This new-old discovery of the impotence of man has been, we are told, "corroborated" by psychologies which "uncover" the emotional dynamics of life. For such psychology, the hunger for security and power, erotic or otherwise, overrides man's reason and turns man into a rationalizer of deep-seated wishes.

Thus, neither man's reason, his will, nor his emotions, according to this theology, can provide a solution to man's anxieties. Back then to the faith of our fathers, back to the Bible, to biblical realism, to evangelical faith; back to the Christian revelation undiluted by Greek reasoning. At the same time, forward to an "encounter" with God which can dispel anxiety and rechannel reason, will, and emotion into the mainstream of a Being unfathomable, who chooses his own ways and his own times to reveal himself to men.

Religious faith in our day is accordingly defined as certainty—albeit an inspired certainty. The promise of faith is in the last analysis a security which comes to one who can "accept" in an "act of faith" beyond understanding. Thus if scientism offers security through limitation, such theology offers security through *fiat.* My conviction is that these ways "out of anxiety" nip off the growing point of the life which pulses uniquely in the religious thrust. They are deceptive byways in the real pilgrimage of faith.

In four chapters I have little space to do justice to opposing views either through attack or concession. I shall set out on what I still consider the main road to mature faith. That road, I believe, at times follows, at other times goes beyond traditional routes. But my purpose here is to speak as simply and directly as I can to the challenge of many students, laymen, and clergymen whom I meet. As I see it, the "difficulties" with religion which so many of them urge stem from an underlying misconception of the way in which religion is imbedded in human life. The approach to the problems of religious living in much theological discussion often stifles their thinking and understanding in terms of the best in their experience. Exposition of the historic faith or "the faith of the Bible," has a way of becoming prematurely dogmatic and normative. It tells one what to expect and how to interpret what happens. Though I would by no means ignore the past, I would approach experience more innocently and let it confirm or outreach the past. We must more persistently let experience talk to reason and reason talk back to experience.

In these four chapters, then, I am trying to cut a trail into four areas which are crucial to personal growth and religious maturity. I am purposely *not* beginning with some important Christian doctrine, for I wish to indicate that basic Christian convictions about life are not imposed from without but that they grow from the very attempt to live deeply and understand as much as possible.

It is the purpose of Chapter 1, therefore, to set the religious pilgrimage within the process of personal growth. In succeeding chapters, I take up core problems which earnest pilgrims face. These are not the only problems, of course, but my hope is that these chapters may lead the reader to greener pastures.

In Chapter 2 I try to show that the problem of evil becomes a stumbling block to religious faith mainly because the more fundamental problem of defining what makes life good has not been carefully thought out. At the root of mature living, Chapter 3 suggests, is the creativity which faces insecurity as the growing-point of life. This unique creativity we know best as love—love which develops into the blessedness of redemptive forgiving.

But is not this quality of living the very heart of the Christian gospel? Must we not realize that the Cross is a symbol of the forgiving Love which defines God's own creative dealing with insecurity? Must we not see that the God to whom Jesus prayed demands a quality of life, indeed a quality of creative fellowship in suffering, which makes life blessed? Must we not understand that in the Christian vision, the insecurity and the suffering in life are not so much removed as redeemed in the ongoing experience of creativity? This fact seems to me to be the fundamental Fact about the cosmos which we call God. And, as Chapter 4 suggests, men at their best will worship a creative, redemptive God, and only this one. Any other they fear. Any other may seem to give security, but not the blessedness which forgiving love knows as creative insecurity.

There are, of course, many other sides to religion and to Christian faith. If what emerges here is a conception of religion as creative insecurity versus "peace of mind," as blessedness versus "happiness," as moral maturity versus psychological "integration," as growth versus "rest," as forgiveness versus prudential goodness, it is because I believe that only a religion which accepts insecurity can destroy evil and purify life. There is a profounder religious psychology than most current psychological treatments of religion seem to realize.

PETER A. BERTOCCI

I

These things I have spoken to you, while I am still with you. But the Counselor, the Holy Spirit, whom the Father will send in my name, he will teach you all things, and bring to your remembrance all that I have said to you. Peace I leave with you; my peace I give to you; not as the world gives do I give to you. Let not your hearts be troubled, neither let them be afraid.

John 14:25-27, Revised Standard Version of *The New Testament*

II

Religion is the vision of something which stands beyond, behind, and within the passing flux of immediate things; something which is real, and yet waiting to be realized; something which is a remote possibility, and yet the greatest of present facts; something that gives meaning to all that passes, and yet eludes apprehension; something whose possession is the final good, and yet is beyond all reach, something which is the ultimate ideal, and the hopeless quest.

The immediate reaction of human nature to the religious vision is worship. . . . The vision claims nothing but worship; and worship is a surrender to the claim for assimilation, urged with the motive force of mutual love. The vision never overrules. It is always there, and it has the power of love presenting the one purpose whose fulfillment is eternal harmony. . . . The power of God is the worship He inspires. . . . The worship of God is not a rule of safety—it is an adventure of the spirit, a flight after the unattainable. The death of religion comes with the repression of the high hope of adventure.

Alfred North Whitehead
Science and the Modern World
(New York: The Macmillan Company, 1925), Chapter XII. Used with the permission of The Macmillan Company.

1

Religion in the Search for Maturity

The Search for God as Insight into Self

For what do we seek when we seek God? How is the search for God related to the deepest cravings we experience? And why do we seek God anyway?

To press these questions is to gain insight into ourselves, for in asking these questions we do not ask what God is in himself, but what part our belief in God is playing in our lives. We are not now asking what our belief in God ought to be, but what we find ourselves seeking as we stand in the midst of good and evil. To be sure, we would soon be asking: Is the God in whom I find myself believing, justified by all the facts of existence as I know them and reason about them? But in this book we shall not be concerned with the grounds for God's existence.[1] We hope, rather, to indicate how our search for God and our thinking about God reflects, and challenges, our growth as persons.

No person becomes mature, we shall see, without taking the religious quest seriously—whatever his final answers may be. What we seek when we seek God is, first and last, an

[1] In *Introduction to the Philosophy of Religion* (New York: Prentice-Hall, 1951) my aim was to advance an adequate argument for God.

answer to the question, What is it that is worth seeking? The minimal religious answer is this: A Being to whose nature our destinies are linked, by whose nature our lives are affected for good, and by whose nature they can be affected even more than they are, if we are properly responsive to that Being. This affirmation may be false, but no person will understand himself, to say the least, unless he takes it seriously enough to ask how it develops. Accordingly, let us first consider two kinds of obstacles that often keep persons from examining the religious quest.

How to Interpret Religious Differences

The first obstacle is the variety of beliefs. Highly intelligent and informed persons thinking about the same ultimate problems come out with vastly different answers. This is true if one compares world religions with each other, but it is also true within one's own religious tradition. There is no minimizing this fact of religious disagreements, or the impact these differences make on the growing mind. How easy it is to be disappointed and confused by the utter seriousness of persons who staunchly defend a variety of beliefs, many of which not only seem weird, but flatly contradictory to each other! As for contradictory behavior—is there any sin in the ingenious human catalogue that has not been committed at some time or other in the name of God?

But what conclusions can be reasonably drawn from this fact of difference in religious beliefs? The conclusion most hostile to religion is that since there is so much confusion about the nature of God, there is no real God outside the beliefs of men. How often have we heard the question: How can anyone believe that there is a God, if there always has been, and still is, disagreement about his nature, both among the learned and the untrained?

Now, of course, it may be that this atheistic conclusion is

true, but I must confess to some surprise that many who hold this view assume that conflicting opinions alone can discredit belief in the existence of God. If this were so, incidentally, the belief that there is no God would be discredited by the same argument, for the counterbeliefs to belief in God are also many. From the fact of difference in belief, about all that follows is that one should sift carefully the evidence upon which he bases his own belief, or unbelief. It follows that each of us should be humble and sensitive to the fact that others may be aware of considerations that have escaped us.

Differences do not mean that each one is equally right. How superficially we move from the view that persons have an equal right to their own convictions to the view that their convictions, though conflicting, are equally right (or correct)! Differences, especially among honest experts, show that it is difficult to know the truth, and that there is more to know.

It is a curious fact, also, that many who would discredit a religious approach to life because it has eventuated in differing conceptions of the same Being, would not think of using the same argument to discredit science. The history of religion is full of conflicting and contradictory views. But so is the history of science. Take, for example, the beliefs of scientific men about the sun and our solar system. Have there not been many conflicting beliefs about it? No scientist would deny the existence of a certain entity—including flying saucers!—*simply* because there has been difference of opinion about it.

What a mature person does in the presence of difference of opinion is to consider the belief in question carefully, with the main different conceptions (hypotheses) in mind. He tries to discover which conception is most consistent with the available facts. The fact of differing opinions makes him humble about his own convictions in any field of thought. But the mature person accepts his intellectual responsibility to weave the many facts of life together into a belief which guides his further thought and action. He makes up his own mind, and tries to live by what he believes, without disregarding the rights of others or new evidence which comes along as he thinks about, and lives by, his conviction. He is not afraid to change his mind. He is only afraid to close his eyes to all the facts. Thus he believes in God, or he believes in atoms, as long as each belief allows all the relevant facts to fall into place.

The belief in God differs from the belief in atoms, and is more difficult to think about. It is also much more important because it is a belief about everything that is, that has happened, and that will happen. We tend to forget that belief in God is a belief that all the other facts and events which occur in history are best explained if we see them as related to the particular belief we have in God. This fact alone should help us to understand why there are more differences in religious belief. Because people differ about what the other facts of life are, and because they differ about what the most important and crucial facts are, they differ in their beliefs about God. Before we come to the last page of this book, this fact will be evident.

But one thing seems clear even at the beginning, when we really stop to think about the matter. We cannot expect religion to make the kind of difference in our lives that is made, quite mechanically, and all at once, when a light is turned on in a dark room. When we press the button, suddenly, all the objects in the room are flooded with the same light, and our eyes easily show us how to make our way from one object to another. This conception of the way religious truth comes seems clearly refuted by the conflict of religious opinions referred to above.

Indeed, without trying in any way to be exhaustive, I want to suggest that our religious convictions are at once part of our growth as personalities, and that they influence the personalities we become. Growth in other beliefs we have has a profound effect on how we think of, and respond to, God. I am not denying the Source of light. To make use of the same figure of speech, I am asking us to remember that the Light is on; there are differences in the eyes that see, and the Light may be used for different purposes.

If we change our figure, we can, perhaps, do more justice to the basic situation we human beings are in. From the time of our birth, mother did all she could to help us. But, as growing children, we both appreciated and failed to appreciate her, in different degrees. At each step of our development we were, no doubt, convinced that we knew the truth about her. But only as we grew into our own maturity did we realize how much our misunderstanding of ourselves and of other events in life led us to misunderstand her. She was there doing her best in the midst of our ventures in living; we easily took her for granted. Much she was trying to do for us we never understood because of our immaturity, or because we would have found it too "inconvenient" to take her seriously.

Is it too much to say that mankind has, in its conviction about God, been in a similar predicament? We shall try to show in these four chapters that our difficulties with God are like our difficulties in relation to our mothers—we misunderstand because, in large part, we do not see our own lives and their ventures clearly, and, sometimes, because we simply do not "dare" to take God seriously. This, at any rate, shall be a guiding idea in this book.

My concern, so far, has been to urge caution in drawing conclusions from the fact of differences in religious belief. But a second obstacle to belief must be dealt with before we start on our main task.

It is argued that belief in a fatherly God is itself a sign of immaturity. As children we come to depend upon our parents for guidance and for love, and we learn to think of home as a place in which our problems will be shared and our suffering soothed. As we get older and face serious problems about the meaning of our little lives, we find it comforting to believe that, far from being lost in a tremendous universe, we are actually in our Home, governed by a loving Father who cares for us when we obey his commands. However, when an adult, facing the complex maze of life, continues to hold this comfortable but childish picture of the universe and his own place in it, he is failing to face the ugly facts about life by "escaping" to this comfortable childish image. He will become emotionally mature only as he relinquishes such infantile wishful thinking, and, realizing that the world is indifferent to any of his dreams and ideals, does his courageous best to get the most out of life.

This type of analysis of religious belief reads like a post-mortem. It proceeds on the assumption that we know the religious venture is an idle one, unsupported by fact. It tells us, indeed, what ails the patient; his religiosity is proof of the fact that he cannot "face" reality.

But persons who speak this way might at least be aware that their own reaction against, or rejection of, religion calls to mind the defiant child who will accept "favors" from nobody. Indeed, whenever we decide to dissolve religious (or other) beliefs simply by psychoanalyzing the individual holding them, we should be thoroughgoing and psychoanalyze ourselves. If we accuse others of rationalizing their sympathies, we should remember that perhaps we too are doing the same thing, or finding excuses to support our antipathies! But assume that the religious person is spoiled in one way, and the antireligious in another. Does it help in finding the truth to explain another's convictions simply as rising from certain emotional needs in him? All conviction or lack of conviction probably has emotional roots. The real question is, Which emotional convictions are best supported by non-emotional considerations? The mature mind does not "emote" about either emotions or ideas. He sets to work finding out the best grounds for accepting or rejecting their validity as guides for his life.

Facing Growth of Religious Meaning

What makes an experience religious

We may begin our constructive analysis by recalling that religion began for us as a matter of beliefs which were later, perhaps, unsettled by the fact that other equally sincere persons held tenaciously to beliefs at variance with our own. Now, though "religion" may have come into *our* lives in church and home as teachings *about* God, that is not the way religion began. And it certainly is not the way religion grows in a human life. Religion, at its core, is a certain kind of *experience of what one believes to be God*. Basically, it is a special *kind* of *prized* experience. During this experience one feels himself to be meeting, to be in a vital relationship to, a Being much greater than himself and anything else he knows.

I am not trying to give an exhaustive account here of the many ways, from time immemorial, in which men have found their God. I am trying to state what probably is the minimum that one feels before the word "religion" or the word "God" comes to mean anything more than a word people use for something or other. People have differed and do differ about what they mean by "God," but persons who believe in "God" because they believe they have *experienced a Presence,* always agree that this experience makes them feel different from all other experiences. They say this "experience of God" has a kind of hold on them which others do not have.

Such persons do not claim to understand completely *what* they experience. They only know that their experience yields a *quality* of existence, a *dimension* of reality, which they have not otherwise known, and which they now treasure. To this experience they have given different names; they have wondered much about it, and they have theorized about whether they could have produced it "all by themselves."

The important point for our attention, however, is this: It is the *experience* of what they come to regard as Supreme in the world that is at the base of their conviction. It matters not how many times one repeats a creed or a prayer. Until he *experiences* something to which this creed and prayer can refer in his life, he is still in what I would call *the pre-experiential stage* of religious development—if it be religious at all! He is like the person who has heard everybody talk about love, "talks" about it himself, but has never *felt* the quality of loving in his own life. We say that he does not "know" what love is until he gets out of this pre-experiential stage and feels it! Similarly with the person who has been brought up "religiously." Sooner or later, if what he has learned about God is to be vital *in* his life, and not simply *to* his life, he will have to compare it to his own experience of the Supreme. This experience of the Supreme is the growing core of religious living as opposed to religious creed. A simple story may clarify what I have in mind:

An eight-year-old boy was sent home from school because he would not repeat the Lord's Prayer with his class. What was taken to be sheer obstinacy and stubbornness by an unsympathetic teacher turned out, upon careful and sympathetic questioning, to be a conflict in the boy's mind between his "creed" and his experience. The Lord's Prayer begins with "Our Father," and it was exactly at this point that the boy "stuck." It came out that the boy's father was a drunkard, cruel to the boy's mother, and more than ill-tempered toward the children. As the boy said: "I don't want to pray to a bad father!" The father of *his experience* did not meet the requirements of the "Father" of his creed.

This simple story, also, can tell us much about the problem that every honest person faces, not only in religion, but in other areas of life. Our lives are full of experiences, experiences of joy and sadness, experiences of many varieties of beauty and ugliness. Experiences, experiences, experiences —some fit in with each other, some conflict with each other, and some simply stand there without our knowing where they fit. Our lives are complex streams of seething experience, and we never really know what the next one is going to be like, though we seldom bother to analyze the differences which actually exist. Most of them are not different enough to cause us much trouble as we label them roughly. But then experiences come along for which we can not find a label; nothing in our stock of words will quite fit. As with the boy, the word "father" came to have a meaning for him which simply could not label the Father "Who art in heaven, hallowed be thy name; thy kingdom come, on earth as it is in heaven." This time the word "Father" did not even fit the emotional meaning that "father" had come to have for him.

If this boy, like other human beings, turned to other non-religious areas of experience he too would find that words he has learned, which others had already coined for the run of their experiences, simply do not fit his own. He would come to realize, on reflection, that in the last analysis, no word, and no thought, can ever be the same as the experience it designates. And he would come to know that we become accustomed to this situation—though we do not realize it—and use the same words even though the experiences we connect with them are so much different from what we started with. Let anyone who doubts this, think of the way in which the same word "mother" has come to be weighted with different experiences from the days of his childhood. The individual does not use a different word, but goes on speaking of "mother" even as he makes his own private mental note of how he "really means" the word. Again, "America," like the symbol "the American Flag," refers in each of our lives to a great variety of experiences. Each of us knows what the word "America" means in a dictionary sense. But the word "America" means to each of us what words can never express. Why? Because for each of us this word now is loaded down with the weight of our own experiences, a load which bursts all the intellectual wrappings we use to transmit our meanings to others.

Many are the words, and many the ideas, then, which grow rich with meaning only if they stop being *mere words* and come to represent shaking experiences. A refugee in one of my classes said to me, with some emotion: "No Americans can know what freedom means. For they do not realize what it means to leave your house in fear to buy groceries, knowing that there is nothing to prevent a car sweeping alongside you as you walk down the street, nothing to prevent your being forced into it, without ever seeing your loved ones again." Freedom meant to this person something which, indeed, Americans forget to remember because it has never *occurred* to them!

If we could now enter into the arena of words and experiences which are much harder to speak of briefly, this thesis would be even better established. One can talk about "beauty" and about "love." But he knows, as he grows older, how hard it is *to tell* what these words stand for in his experience. They each start off as words we learn from others, but they take on their load of meaning only as we come to experience what *we* take to be beauty, and what love stirs within *us*.

Such oversimplified discussion must suffice to illustrate this step in religious maturity; the realization that our words, our thoughts, and our creeds will never say completely for each of us, or for all of us, what the experience of "God" will mean in our lives. And if "God" continues to mean a word learned from someone else's speech, a word that does not speak also of our own experience, then we have not yet moved from the pre-experiential to the *experiential* stage of religious development. As part of this stage, we must realize that the same word will "say" different things to us as we go on experiencing, because the word is more than a dictionary word; it is a word for *our* experience.

Unless we remember this fact, we shall be open to the same disaster confronting a college senior who recently came for counsel concerning her love "for a boy of a different religion." When asked what God meant to her, she said: "Oh, it means the celestial Being, who, when I was six years old, helped me to get across the street safely, a 'Someone' who takes care of us, supposedly, but I have no clear ideas about him." This was her "God." But questioning brought out that the boy she wanted to marry used the word "God" for a Comrade to whom he prayed regularly, and in whom he felt a constant companion in joy, in sorrow, in aspiration. Her religion, her "God," had withered and was dead; his "God" was an experience of comradeship in every venture of life. The unfortunate fact in this situation was not, presumably, that two persons of different religions wanted to get married. It consisted in the fact that this young man would find out that the person he loved did not love the "God" who led her across the street at the age of six, the "God" so different in her life from his God.

Keeping words married to experiences

This story illustrates another phase of this same transition from pre-experiential to experiential religious maturity. Words, we have just seen, are like a bottle which can be used for more than one liquid. As we grow older, we use the same bottles for a varying content of experiences. We cannot communicate with each other—nor could we with ourselves—without words. And there is no use supposing that it will ever be otherwise, namely, that the words which stand for vital experiences in our lives will ever be able to express exactly the growth of experience. *In this sense,* life is always· deeper than logic, as we often hear.

This, however, does not give anybody the right to be illogical, or to renounce the responsibility for being as clear as he can about his experiences and their relations to each other. It rather serves to warn us that we should always look beyond words and their logical relationships to see what experiences these words are trying to bottle up for distribution. We should not suppose that we understand what other people mean by some of the same words we use until we are aware of what phase of experience they are using the words to describe. "God" meant to the young woman a kind of being her sweetheart had long outgrown. He actually did not believe in her God; and she had a *word* for his belief but did not have the *experience* to put into the word as he used it.

How much unnecessary religious conflict would be avoided if we could remember this fact! A student says that he does not believe in prayer. It turns out that he does not believe in constantly petitioning for little favors from God, and that he detests "bargaining" with God—"If Thou wilt save me from this situation, I promise that in the future I will never do this again." If this were *all* that prayer has meant to persons or to any one person, the disbeliever could be satisfied that in rejecting "prayer" he had rejected a childish belief. But such an idea of prayer does not fit the prayer-experience of mature religious persons. The Lord's Prayer, for example, belies this conception of prayer. What has happened to this "disbeliever"? He has allowed the word to capture only one kind of experience, but, nevertheless, used that word as the only standard of what anybody would mean by "prayer." As a matter of fact, mature religious people almost never use the word "prayer" simply for petition and never for "bargaining."

As our insight into our own experience deepens, then, we

realize that there is a constant interaction going on between our experiences and our labels for these experiences. As our experience grows and changes, we do not always use a new word (as in the case of "mother"), but we keep the same word for the fuller experience. It is not, however, a one-way process of unconsciously forcing different experiences into the same bottle. Often, without realizing it, we judge the contents of the bottle by the shape of the bottle, and choose or avoid experiences by what we think the bottle holds. The adolescent who is "through with love," because of a disappointing experience with a member of the opposite sex, is an excellent example of the way one experience of "love" can poison the mind. The maturing religious person realizes that he needs both words and experiences and must keep checking them with each other.

Expression of religious feeling in ritual, art, and myth

Fortunately, words are only one way we have of expressing our experiences. We use words not only to stabilize and order our experiences for ourselves, but especially to communicate with others. But, as we have seen, our words are far from successful in performing their function because our living experiences outreach our wording of them.

Actually, before words came to be possible for us, we "expressed ourselves" not in words, but in cries, gestures, and bodily movements—and we still do when we find that words will not meet the demands of our experiences. Whenever we are "overwhelmed" by some deep feeling, do we not find ourselves using what seem the "natural" physical gestures and movements to "say" what we feel (although I suspect that most of the time we would identify the movement with the experience)?

Again, it is not my purpose here to expound any exhaustive theory of how our actions are related to our experiences. But it is vital to realize that we, all of us, have found and do find ways of using our bodies and the world around us (as well as words) to "express" what we have felt. We talk about the "right" gesture just as we talk about the "right" word; and we are critical of the dancer or the singer who seems to be going "through an act" rather than "feeling" what he is doing or singing. The rich variety of artistic forms, from painting through poetry, song, architecture, sculpture, and the dance—all are ways in which human beings have been trying to "express" their varied experiences of life. Such expression is necessary both as a part of the experience they are undergoing, and also as a way of communicating to others something about life they hold to be significant. Just as a word may "hold up" an experience for others to see— but may also be the very way of completing or pointing up the experience—so the colored strokes on a canvas, the rhythmic sway of a body, may be a way of "finishing off" what is felt, as well as calling the attention of others to something felt to be important and worth experiencing.

We have been saying that we can never find the "right" word or verbal description for many stirring and prized experiences in our lives. Perhaps artistic expression and ritual do more justice to what we feel we have undergone, and we are glad to let certain actions be *symbolic* of what we have felt. It is in this way that we must understand some of the great *myths,* such as the Story of Adam and Eve, or Cain and Abel. To think of these stories as false is to forget that stories are truer than historical fact when they depict for us a situation we constantly confront as human beings, even though we do not go through the same actions as those described in the story told. Again, a great "myth" is not historically true, but it is true to life for those who see that it speaks to the drama of their lives significantly.

Because religion deals with the very meaning of the prized events in human experience, we should expect to see *through* the words, *through* the rituals, *through* the myths, *through* the artistic symbol by which people try to express these dramatic events.

Indeed, Professor William Ernest Hocking has insisted that "religion is the mother of the arts," that "all the arts of common life owe their present status and vitality to some sojourn within the historic body of religion." [2] This figure of religious experience as a fertile mother, as a matrix within which the other phases of life gain nourishment, is suggestive of the way in which religious influence can work in our lives; for it seems clear to me that a person who has felt what he calls the "presence of God" finds this experience spreading its effect on the rest of his personality and the rest of his pursuits and values. This is evident from the history of human experience with religion.

But another thing seems equally clear, and equally important, if we are to be fair to all the facts. Potent as it is, the religious experience has from the beginning been one experience among others, has had to compete with other members of the family of human experiences. As such a member, it has been used by other experiences *for their purposes as well as having transformed them for its purposes.* Even this statement of constant interaction between the various facets of human experience is inadequate, for it is nearer the truth to say that from the very beginning the religious experience has seemed to speak with many voices to many people. Why? *Because from the very beginning in each life the religious moment has had to "speak" in a voice which the experient would understand in the light of his more ordinary experiences and his habits of living.* Thus, in some lives, if there is any religious consciousness at all, it seems to be in the dim and feeble background; in other lives it seems to be the servant of other interests deemed more important. And even when it seems dominant, when it stirs earthquaking

[2] William E. Hocking, *The Meaning of God in Human Experience* (New Haven, Conn.: Yale University Press, 1916), p. 14 and p. 13.

responses in a given life, it is often forced to make itself effective through the moral, aesthetic, and practical interests of the person involved. No doubt, as we shall now see, this is part of the reason that religion is easily identified with each of these—sometimes with the good life, sometimes with the dedication to beauty—as if it were no more than goodness or beauty. And these interests often seem to ";co-operate" with religion only when they have conformed it to their needs. We may see more vividly how this works if, in what follows, we try to construct a rough sample of what takes place in our lives as we grow in religious maturity. Let us be clear, however, at the outset, that the actual process of religious challenge and growth is much more complicated than this oversimplified sketch.

How threat to survival may affect religious belief

Man is a striving being, a fighter for ends, as William James called him. It is easy to think of him as a more adjustable, complicated animal, whose main concern is to eat, exercise, sleep, and procreate. Let us suppose, as a first stage, that this is all man is—except that he *knows that he wants to preserve himself,* and also knows, what animals do not know, that he can be hurt, and can die. How would a person who conceived his life thus, in terms of physical satisfaction, avoidance of pain, and continuance of his comfortable status with as much security as possible, be tempted to interpret experiences "of God's presence," assuming that he could have such experience? Would he not relate this experience of "God" to his master-desire for food? Since he wants his food supply to be constant, and since he wants his life to be preserved against danger, both from the uncertain dangers of a physical nature and from "his enemies," he may well cry out with the Psalmist, "The Lord shall preserve thy going out and thy coming in from this time forth, and even for evermore" (Psalm 131:8).

For such a person, in other words, the first requirement for God to be "God," and worthy of worship, is that "God" keep him safe and well-fed. And this, after all, is understandable enough! For instance, what demand do children make upon their fathers and mothers more naturally than their demand for physical sustenance and protection? This person who never gets beyond his demand for physical security is, at a lower level perhaps, still one with all the rest of us who insist that no Being can be declared good or worthy of worship, unless He protects us sufficiently to allow us to survive with a safe margin of security.

That would be an interesting tale which dramatized for us the multitudinous ways in which this interpretation of "God," as the Preserver of our physical health and safety, has manifested itself in the lives of men. If, however, we scrutinize our own lives, especially in times of danger, we may find a strong analogy in our spontaneous outcry that God protect us and our loved ones. When we find ourselves wishing for a "miracle," do we not do so in the conviction that God may, or at any rate *should,* alter the laws of nature in order to protect us in our physical emergencies? Just as the child cannot understand why his father cannot do many things which the child feels necessary to his welfare, just as the child frequently considers his father mean and unfair, so the children of God fall easy prey to the assumption that of course God can do anything for them in their need, that he can add and subtract to the world as he wills, that he can suspend any of the laws of Nature.

If one begins with this conception of a "Father," two things may happen when God does not answer prayers for physical succor. The "believer" may become discouraged and stop believing in God. In other words, whenever he has any thought or emotional intimation that there is a God, he will dismiss it as a "false alarm," no longer to be trusted. The believer becomes a disbeliever. Yet this need not take place, for a "believer" may reflect that he himself has somehow incurred the wrath of God and that God has withheld his blessing, until he has made the proper sacrifice or restitution. Remembering the blessings of the past, the believer may not give up his belief in God altogether, but decide that God is not showering good upon him because he has been ungrateful and disobedient.

No reader of the early chapters of Genesis can miss this motif in the expulsion of Adam and Eve from the Garden of Eden. There in the Garden all of Adam's and Eve's needs for survival were satisfied without their labor or suffering. That man must now have to gain sustenance by the sweat of his brow, that woman should, in begetting children, experience the pains of childbirth, these facts are explained by the fundamental fact that man disobeyed the will of God. But only a person who conceived of work as undesirable, or of pain as necessarily bad, and who conceived of "Heaven" as a Garden of Eden in which man had neither pain nor labor, could give such an account.

I am not forgetful of the grandeur of these early accounts in Genesis in other respects, but this hedonistic element in the outlook of one of the writers cannot escape us—simply because it is still so influential in much of our own thinking about God. God, so many believe, will do anything to preserve us in health and to protect us from pain if only we do his will aright, and make proper restitution for past error; for God is the Power of Life, the Creator whose impenetrable will is the basic source of our physical health. Every attempt on the part of man, since the beginning of human striving, to win the favor of God, be it by incantation and dance, by the sacrifice of animals, and even of human beings, in order to have "God" on man's side, takes root in this basic conviction that God is the Giver of health and security, especially to those who obey his will. Nor are these rituals, sacrificial and otherwise, simply additions to the religious experience; they are not merely maneuvers for convincing God, though this motive too, no doubt, was often involved. But essentially these rituals were expressions of the plight men felt themselves to be in; they were part of a tremendous experience of a world which they felt had a deeper meaning.

Religious experience and the development of moral insight

The Old Testament is replete with illustrations of this interpretation of God as Protector and Defender of the obedient. Is He not the protector and defender of the Jewish people, the God who promised after the Flood never to visit "his people" again with this kind of punishment? But, as we have hinted, we do not find this conception starkly separated from any other. It is usually accompanied by, and interrelated with, another "meaning" which "God" comes to have in the experience of men. Indeed, even in the conception of God as Preserver and Defender, we see man's moral ideas and ideals taking shape and determining how he thinks of God's relation to him.

To begin with, a man may start with the natural expectancy and assurance that just because he is alive in the world, the world not only does and will, but *ought to* take care of him—just as the infant moves from assurance that his parents will take care of his physical needs to the assumption that they ought to! As we have said, when disappointment is keen, the child may become bitter and cynical, and the "believer" may deny the existence of any Providence. But he who goes on believing does so by introducing a *moral relation* as the basis for security and insecurity! He himself accepts some (and usually all) of the responsibility himself for the breakdown in "protection." He decides that he has incurred the wrath of God because he has not acted in a manner befitting him as God's creature. Again, however else we may interpret the story of Adam's and Eve's disobedience, the underlying current is that Adam and Eve acted as if the Garden of Eden were theirs, for them to use as *they* pleased. This basic attitude, that the world is man's for him to use as if he were its owner, is condemned over and over again, by the moral-religious mind. It is God's world, and men ought to live in it according to God's will. Then they do not suffer.

In the "myth" of Cain and Abel this religious theme becomes more subtle morally, for now we see the writer facing the problem: What is the attitude which two successful men ought to take toward the world? Are they to take their blessings for granted even when they themselves have worked hard for them? Cain, the successful farmer, seemed to take the attitude: "I have worked hard for my possessions, so why should I give my very best as an offering to God? Indeed, since this is the sweat of my brow, and not any handout, I have every right to distribute it as I wish." So he "brought of the fruit of the ground an offering unto Jehovah" (Genesis 4:3); to the Protector and Defender he brought a kind of rent, to be paid with something less than gratitude!

His brother Abel, however, "brought of the firstlings of his flock and the fat thereof" (Genesis 4:4). Perhaps he reasoned to himself, "No matter how much I have labored, my blessings would have been impossible without the help of God who created both the world and me. To him belong the best products of my labor, as a token of my gratitude." Can we legitimately read into his actions this attitude? Cain's action seemed reluctant, grudging; Abel's, generous and eager.

The story, however, goes on to impress us with another set of *moral* relations besides that of responsible gratitude toward God as a basis for God's favor; for it goes on to tell us how Cain "was very wroth" because God had no "respect" for his offering, and how he took it out on his brother Abel whom he slew. When God asked Cain where his brother

Abel was, Cain not only lied, but his self-centeredness led him to ask in his own defense: "Am I my brother's keeper?" (Genesis 4:9). God's condemnation was swift: "When thou tillest the ground, it shall not henceforth yield unto thee its strength; a fugitive and a wanderer shalt thou be in the earth" (Genesis 4:12).

Here, clearly, the motif of God as Providence is tied in with the moral understanding that not only is man to be properly grateful to God for a world in which his labors can yield sustenance and abundance, but that not even these goods will be assured unless man assumes responsibility for his brother. God is now conceived as the ordainer of justice among men.

Once more, I am not urging these interpretations of biblical episodes as definitive. Nevertheless, I see in them stages in the evolution of religion which can be corroborated in our own evolution as persons.[3] Part of the genius and appeal of these stories is the fact that they remind us dramatically of our own religious development as persons, for each of us needs to explore and understand the meaning of his own many and varied emotional responses to the world in which he lives. The world bears in on us as physical beings, faced by hunger, pain, and death, and finds us convinced of a Power who is not indifferent and who cares, provided we too care and are obedient.

Our physical needs, however, are saturated with other kinds of uneasiness and yearning. As human beings we do not, like animals, live unreflectively with each other. We ask: "What is our relation to each other both in times of emergency and in times of peace? Are there laws purposed by Providence which govern these relations? Does He expect us to be grateful to him, our Keeper, without expecting us to care for the man who works in the neighboring field?" And

[3] A brief and interesting description and interpretation of the development of the moral consciousness may be found in Chapter I of A. C. Garnett, *The Moral Nature of Man* (New York: The Ronald Press, 1953).

we reply: "No, the God who made the laws of physics and the laws of biology did not leave off there; so he expects men —he does not force them, evidently—to care for each other, and not treat themselves as privileged characters. In his eyes, justice among men is the norm, and to destroy this law is to court disaster."

It takes much development, however, to move from a low morality which concerns itself with physical security, to the norm of Western civilization: "Thou shalt love the Lord thy God with all thy heart, with all thy soul, with all thy strength, and with all thy mind, and thy neighbor as thyself!" This First Commandment speaks not only of God as the Provider of the physical needs of men but as the Defender of men against each other's hate, and the Sponsor of good will. Nevertheless both religion and morality grow as man's conception of his social needs and responsibilities are tied in with, as well as inspired by, his unique experience of a Presence—a Presence which now makes itself known to him not only through wind and fire, through sunrise and harvest glow, but also through the experiences he has with his fellow men. This same interweaving of the moral with the religious, this gradual increase of insight into the nature of both man and God, is found in the "myth" of Job. In this grand and moving allegory, we come to a high point in moral-religious evolution and complexity. The question now is, How shall we understand suffering and the loss of one's possessions? Is it always punishment for unrighteousness and disobedience to God's will?

Religious experience and suffering

The reader will recall that, according to The Book of Job,[4] Satan, impressed by the goodness of Job, scoffingly

[4] The reader is reminded that the account here given of Job's problem would need considerable qualification if it purported to be a scholarly analysis of the Book for its own sake.

says to God that Job has every reason to be good, since he has a good family, good health, and more than his share of worldly possessions. It was "paying" Job to be good, so, why not? Now, after all, we would expect Satan to demean the motives of a good man; we often do it ourselves when we say, "Every man has his price," or suggest that "he wouldn't be good, if—."

The writer of The Book of Job, however, is convinced that men are not good just because of some external reward. Nor is he convinced that the evil that occurs in men's lives can be entirely explained as punishment for evil-doing. Both views, he thinks, are oversimplified views of the matter. Thus he has God confidently take up Satan's challenge and allows him to afflict Job with every evil and torture possible, short of death. Satan attacks Job's supposed sources of goodness, beginning with the loss of his physical possessions, proceeding to the destruction of his loved ones, then attacking Job's own health, and even creating a situation in which Job's mental anguish becomes greater than his physical suffering. Job, afflicted with his own personal loss and unremitting suffering, must also ask why innocent loved ones, for whom he would give his own life, had to be lost. Nor can he, in honesty, escape the question: "Can it be that I have done something to warrant these afflictions to myself and to them?"

The simplest answer, for a believer in God, would be to exonerate God and place all the blame on man. If a believer insists upon the justice of God, then, since it would be unjust of God to inflict suffering which is not deserved, the sufferer simply *must* have perpetrated some evil! And this is exactly the stand taken by Job's conventional friends, who represent the simplest answer in this predicament. They plead with Job to confess his secret sin, to repent of the evil which has brought total suffering into his life. Indeed, they add to Job's torture by suggesting that he is being less than honest with himself about his innocence.

Here it is that Job's stand takes us, at one grand stroke, beyond much conventional morality and conventional religion. Here it is that Job opens another moral-religious possibility which has inspired many sensitive minds who have read his story, for Job will not blacken his own motives or his own conduct when the most honest scrutiny of which he is capable does not justify self-condemnation. He can simply stand and say humbly but firmly: "I have done no evil, and certainly none to deserve this!"

How many *good* men have stood exactly at this point! Racked by pain and loss that exceeded, by any reasonable standard, the measure of justice, they and their friends have asked: Is this fair? If such loss and suffering are to be the lot of the good as well as the bad, is this a universe that cares a whit about what men do? Is it not more bearable, as well as more reasonable, to believe that man is alone in his struggle for goodness and security, that he is to expect no aid for special effort? Better, then, to believe that the world is indifferent to men, for to believe that God cares is to court disaster and the despair of feeling let-down. Let's rid ourselves of all futile expectations and stop blaming or praising a universe that cannot either know or feel the plight of man!

Is there any way beyond these alternatives: (a) evil is deserved punishment, (b) evil is misfortune which one must expect in an indifferent world? In our next chapter we shall look at these questions more constructively. Here, we must note that both these answers are in reality guided by the same moral conviction, namely, that the world is not unfair to a good man. The first decision simply says that man is not good, that he deserves the evil which comes to him. The second decision may well be based on the conviction that since it is intolerable to suppose that a cosmic Power should inflict evil on undeserving men, it is better to believe that the universe is neither good nor bad, that is, that there is no caring God.

Job's own final answer is not a neat one, but it is a great one (much as I cannot grant that it will do in every respect); for Job will not denigrate man, and he will not denigrate the universe. Thus, in the end, though tortured by suffering from which death would be a welcome deliverance, he does not deny that God cares. Nor does he assert that the evil that has come to him is something he deserves. He simply affirms that God can be trusted with his fate, that there is some reason for his suffering which he cannot fathom, and that God is worthy of his allegiance and trust even when evil occurs which he cannot understand!

What possible reasons can Job have for this attitude? Two points must not escape us as we reflect upon this matter. First, though Job does not tell us in so many words, it may at least be inferred that he is aware that whatever good he has experienced in life he has experienced in this world. His pain is all the more acute because he has known the blessings open to man. Here he is on Abel's side, aware of, and sensitive to, the fact that he must not, as a moral creature, take his blessings for granted, that it is beneath gratitude to forget the good that has occurred when it is swept away. Every human being should face, in other words, the problem of goodness beyond desert, as well as the problem of evil beyond desert. Man faces both the problem of undeserved good and the problem of undeserved evil, and the mature man cannot deny or minimize the basic fact that unless he knew goodness he could not mourn its loss. It is this fact that is so important in the consciousness of many persons that no matter what happens they, with Whittier, cannot believe that they can ever pass "beyond His love and care."

Second, fully aware of such goodness, such persons are all the more grateful for the many experiences of exaltation when it seems indeed that "my cup runneth over." In this mood they have said: "God's in his heaven and all's right with the world." This feeling does not leave men easily, and it did not leave Job. He had in a fundamental sense *experienced* the goodness of life and the universe, and the measure was such that even when he could not understand, he could be faithful and think only the best of God.

Religious experience as moral fellowship with God

Here, clearly, we have moved to a more subtle and deeper level of living, and the religious experience both supports and is interpreted by this clearer awareness of man's moral struggle and blessing. Graciousness, generous feeling, trust which believes in the supremacy of the best even when the destruction of past good seems to be all that remains, these replace tit-for-tat justice, or the search for one's own security. One now lives in the universe not as a spoiled child, or an ungracious one, counting up deserts, and being sure that the balance between give-and-take is meticulously kept. He lives, maturely, *with* God, sharing good and evil, but never making the amount and the balance the only or the main consideration. Here is the religion of moral fellowship, of mutual appreciation, of trust and faith. Such religious fellowship with God, far from being blind to facts of evil, is sensitive to the deeper fact that we live creatively, never by merely keeping a moral score card, but always by simply playing the game co-operatively.

The mother of the ten-year-old boy who was taken from her by a malignant disease knew something her neighbors and even her pastor did not yet appreciate. As they all stood by the grave, amid the crying of relatives and the solemn faces of stunned friends, she asked for the opportunity to pray. The momentary quiet was made holy by her prayer: "Dear God, thank you for the joy which Jimmy brought into my life; help me to keep the memory of his love, and to be worthy of it as long as there is life in me."

Moral Maturity and Religious Belief

What we have tried to suggest in this chapter is that religion in most of human life is ultimately rooted in our maturing experience of what we call the goodness of life. Much of what religion means to us will depend on our own moral growth. We have tried to show that these feelings which convince us that our God lives, are experiences which are constantly interpreted in the light of our conception of what life is all about. It is not that religion is simply dependent on the other phases of life; it is not that it can never escape entanglement with them; it is simply that all these aspects of life forever mingle with each other. The human being has many needs, interests, and sensitivities, each of which can enslave and be enslaved by the other, but no one of which succeeds, as a rule, in silencing the other. As we have seen, the person seeking physical security may soon find himself *justifying* his search or enlarging it, for moral reasons! The person who seeks one level of moral security may soon find himself with a new vision of what morality is. At the very same time, a person in seeming to give himself to one quest finds that quest giving way to another. To use a crude analogy, a man starts eating with one stomach, but what he eats changes the stomach he will eat with; and, let us say, he finds himself with new tastes and new power. He may say or even think that all he wants is food, but he soon finds that food he takes from another somehow does not taste as good as food which he has honestly earned.

At each step of life, then, a man's religion will reflect his total development, achievement, and maturity. What he calls his religion will hardly stand still if he is growing in other respects. At the same time, as his religious appreciation grows, it sheds its inspiration and perspective on the remainder of his efforts. The religious effort, accordingly, is knit into the whole of human striving for "the things that matter most." It works with them, is often enslaved by them, but it also can drive them to new heights of achievement. Often its destiny may seem to be in bondage to the rest of man's life, but careful analysis also finds it inspiring the whole of a man's existence by its effort to plumb the meaning of that Presence to which his responsive feelings and his thinking so often point. Morality which loses the inspiration of the religious search for the further meaning of the Presence loses the fire it needs to grow. Without religious passion morality tends to become "moralistic"; rule and precept take the place of spiritual growth; the hot star becomes cold stone. The religious man wants to be not only "at one" with the power in things; he not only wants to find his proper relation to his fellow men, but he hungers with all his heart, and mind, and strength, to be at one with God. His knowledge and his morality grow out of, are part of, his search for God.

Thus it should never surprise us to find variety in religion, even the variety which means contradiction (though this does not mean that we should be satisfied with contradiction). The religious effort will reflect one's personal development, achievement, and conviction in every area of life, at the same time that it expresses the human concern that man's good be in harmony with, and thus protected by, what is felt to be the inner Presence of all things.

A last word of warning: In this first chapter I have tried to present the religious situation in man's life, not in all its aspects, but in terms of aspects which are central to the religious venture as I am convinced most of us find it. It may be that we can now better understand why religion can be so varied, so pervasive in the lives of men, and also so unified. But we can also see how it can be connected with orgies, exuberances, and exaggerations of every sort even as it inspires serenity, high purpose, and the noblest living. I am increasingly convinced that a big mistake in our thinking about religion is the one we make when we think of the religious aspect of man's life (or the moral, or the aesthetic, or the physical) as some sort of fixed deposit with certain prescribed content.

Man's life is a persistent unity of seeking and understanding and appreciating. Man does not know his own full potentialities, any more than he knows what the world is. He interprets himself and that world in the light of his promptings and varied responses. His deep-rooted layers of emotional striving, his religious *experience,* his moral *experience,* his aesthetic *experience,* his biological *experience,* his intellectual *experience,* are all part of his total responsiveness; and all contribute to the meaning of each other and to his conception of the universe in which he lives and the life he ought to live in it. To achieve maturity in religion, I am convinced, is to remind oneself constantly of this fact and to demand growth in every area of life. Then our formulations will not be taken as "the last word"; nor will our experiences be left unprotected without formulation or appropriate action.

To achieve maturity in religion, we must achieve maturity in our thinking, feeling, and action in the other phases of life. We shall not achieve maturity, however, in other areas if we ignore our sense of the tie which binds us to the rest of reality and to the best in reality—God. Yet who of us, in our search for the worth while, has never stood where Job did, or even felt as the student I am about to mention in the next chapter did? Jesus warned his disciples not to pour new wine into old bottles (Matthew 9:17), and he also reminded them that they were not ready for much he would like to share with them.

2

Religion as the Pursuit of Creativity by God and Man

Can a Good God Allow Evil? [1]

He looked me square in the eye, and his eyes were flames of indignation. "Your God is a fool!"

Thus spoke a university student. He was not "another cynical, callow youth." I knew him well enough to recognize his passion for social justice. It was moral earnestness which led to this eruption, and it is only fair that I summarize the rest of his case.

"You tell me," he said in substance, "that God knew that men would oppress other men, that men would consider it great fun to see other men torn alive by lions in a Coliseum, that they would feel victorious when they systematically killed six million Jews, that they would take advantage of each others' weaknesses in every conceivable way, in slum, in sweatshop, and in segregated schools—you tell me that he knew that this could and probably would happen; you tell me that he could have avoided this by making men differently, but that, nevertheless, he did make them as they

[1] A portion of this chapter appeared in slightly different form in *Motive*, 1956, under the title "Is God a Fool?"

are, capable now of exploding the very earth in each others' faces. Sir, I repeat, your God is a fool!"

Many students I have known have been less forthright, but they have been equally decisive. I can still feel the surprised and indignant incredulity of the Negro college girl whose every word accused me of moral blindness when she said: "How can you say that God is just when he knew what having a black skin would mean to so many human beings?"

At moments like these I am glad that there was a day in my own life when I too was similarly overwhelmed by "man's inhumanity to man," for I now can feel with such students and be glad that their sense of fair play speaks, no matter how misguided. But, if I were now to be equally forthright I would say, with equal passion, I suspect, "Any other God *would* be a fool!"

And, I would continue: "If God made man so that he could not hurt others, if God had made man in such a way that he could never choose to create a slum, a concentration camp, and an atomic inferno, he would be unworthy of the name, and certainly not worthy of the worship of a *mature moral person!*"

The issue is now sharply joined. And as the three italicized words emphasize, the argument turns on what we mean by a mature moral person. When the student said he thought that God was a fool if he could prevent the evil men did to each other, but did not, what was he really saying? He was saying that he could not understand how any Being could be morally justified in allowing a situation to occur which could eventuate in the kind of suffering, and the amount of suffering, which human beings inflict upon each other. What he was denouncing was my conception of what made life worth while. When he attacked the idea of God he was really asserting his own set of values, by which God was falling short.

What is the premise on which I base a defense of the God which my student so indignantly rejected? It is the conviction that God's fundamental purpose for man's life is that man should be free to use his God-given abilities to do good, or to do evil. It was not God's purpose that man *do* evil, but it was God's purpose that he be allowed, that he be free, to do evil. This would mean that man could oppose God's purpose and actually use his God-given abilities to work against His own will as far as those abilities allowed. God, in other words, did not make men as a puppet maker creates his puppets; he did not make them to act "on the strings" which he alone controlled.

There is a sense, of course, in which men are puppets. Men, like puppets, can use only the capacities which constitute their nature. But they are unlike puppets in two important ways. In the first place, they are not just "made," once for all time, but their capacities develop, and the course of the development depends in good measure upon the choices they themselves make. In the second place, they are not compelled to develop their capacities in one direction only, to one foreordained conclusion. No man is forced to develop his mind to its utmost capacity. What is more, he does not have to come to one and only one conclusion. Or, even had it been ordained that he come to a certain conclusion, he would not be forced to do anything about it! In a word, God presumably could have made man like a machine that smoothly operates, with all its power, only in one way, and only when the proper button is pressed. And man could therefore have been a kind of automatic machine, with compassion and good will "built in," who would interact with his fellow men but never hurt them. On the view I am expounding, however, God believed that it was better not to preordain such compassion.

Having said this, I can hear the student cry once more: "But why? Why make persons in such a way that they can hurt themselves and each other, if you can help it? Surely, we would consider any man a fool who made his children so that they could destroy each other, if he could avoid it? Why change this verdict when it is God, who, presumably, could have done otherwise?"

We are back again! But we are now nearer to the basic issue. Would we condemn such a father? I think the answer is clear: *Yes, provided that in making it impossible for his children to hurt and destroy each other, he at the same time made it impossible for them to have other experiences which make life worth while.* The argument thus will turn on the answer to another question. Let it be clear that neither the student nor I are "for" suffering; we are both "against" it! But the assumption in his thinking is that one could avoid this suffering without making impossible "the things that matter most" in life.

The fundamental issue, then, does not immediately concern the nature of God. It concerns the nature of significant human living. We must ask two questions. First, what experiences in human life make living worth while? And, second, so far as one can know, can we enjoy these experiences without at the same time confronting the risks of falling into evil ourselves, and of hurting others?

The issue is so important that I restate it. I am suggesting that we cannot be clear about what we mean by God's goodness until we become clearer about the nature of the good in human life. Many thoughtful persons doubt the goodness of God because they disapprove of what they see in human beings who are his handiwork. In so doing, they are judging the actions of man and of God by a standard of goodness which I think should be rejected. In any case, we cannot be clear in asserting or denying: "God is good to man," until we decide what it is that, so far as we can tell, makes life good.

Let me then state what I think makes life worth while, or good. Here I can do little more than suggest a line of thought which is not merely my own. I have been especially influenced by what seems to me to be the best in the Graeco-Judeo-Christian tradition—in other words, in the thought and action of Socrates, Plato, Aristotle, the Stoics, the Hebrew Prophets, Jesus, Paul, St. Augustine, St. Francis, St. Thomas Aquinas, Spinoza, Kant, and Hegel. I could, of course, mention others and I must not give the false impression that even these men are all on one level of agreement, or greatness. I mention them because, in one way or another, it seems to me that each has put a finger on what it is that gives human life dignity and worth. And, without mentioning names, I shall make use of certain rewarding trends of investigation and thought in recent psychology as I make a detour to the central question of what constitutes God's goodness.

What Makes Human Life Worth While?

We need to be loved.

So many are the meanings of the word "love" that I almost hesitate to say that human life would not be worth while without the *experience of love*. But no other word in our language will better indicate the area of life I have in mind. Love comes into our lives in different ways, reflecting the degree of maturity we have at the time. But, and this will be my thesis, love comes into our lives as the protector both of our freedom and of our security. To tell the story of love in each of our lives is to tell the story of how we developed our capacity for our freedom and security. It may be that in what follows I can clarify my meaning enough to justify my conviction that no other good in life is greater than love, for love at its best is at once the expression of our creativity as human beings and the protector of our creativity.

Most of us have known the love of mother and father. Their love was there before we knew what it was. We learned the meaning of our own emotions in the context of their responses to us. We learned what our states of anger, of fear, of gratitude, of jealousy meant, in large part through the way they dealt with us when we experienced these states. They taught us what sounds to leave out of our baby talk, what syllables to accent, and which of our enunciations would communicate to others what we were wanting and thinking. Bit by bit, by their example and direction in most of the emotional nooks and crannies of our lives, we learned what emotions we should prefer, and how we were expected to express them or any thoughts we wanted to convey. Listen to the little girl scolding her baby doll, notice what it is she scolds the doll for, mark the punishment doled out, and you will probably find the girl enacting her conception of mother's and father's tactics with her.

As each of us grew older we put those values on things which our parents (or those who stood in their place as guides), put on experiences; and we even came to evaluate ourselves in the light of what we thought was their evaluation of us. In inexpressible ways we were dependent upon them, and, more than we realized, we fitted our actions to the patterns which we thought they would approve. In fact, our sense of security and self-confidence grew in accordance with our conception of how well we were pleasing them. Of course, I am assuming that in these early days we were fortunate enough to have parents who cared about us and who did not treat us like furniture, to be kept clean and in its place.

Our dependence upon parents and others was due to the fact that we were not born with the capacity to take care of ourselves. For most of us our behavior, as we matured, was not fixed in one pattern. As human infants we were wonderously flexible. But this very flexibility was the source of our dependence upon mother and father. And if mother and father knew enough, and "put their minds to it," they could have gone a long way toward making their flexible infants become little automatons—not to say well-tamed circus animals almost unerringly responsive to the crack of the whip or the tone of the voice.

Anyone who has seen the child who dares not leave its mother's side, who breaks into tears at the slightest reprimand, and flushes with pleasure at a kind word, knows how far this process of "training" can go. Now, if this child had simply the capacities of an animal, or if it could not soon observe that other persons do things differently, or realize that mother herself is quite inconsistent at times, the damage done by such training would be negligible (as with animals). For the less ability and flexibility a person has, the better, perhaps, it is for him to live "in a rut." The point is that parents who train the plastic abilities and emotions of their children into certain grooves are—like the tamers of circus animals—not interested in the child for his own sake, but only in controlling what will happen to him. They may even plead that they are anxious to avoid trouble, both for themselves, for others, and for the child. Indeed, they are interested in the child's doing the "approved" thing.

Such training, and the motivation behind it, seems very sensible on the surface, for it prevents wrongdoing and encourages safety. We should all agree, no doubt, that some actions, especially those that concern his own immediate physical health and that of others, must be demanded for the child's own sake. But the real problem in child training is the same problem we must face if we are to answer the question before us. Do we train the child just for the sake of training him, or do we teach him so that he will preserve and increase the possibilities of value in his life? Do we teach or train him so that he will, as soon as possible—and this applies even to basic safety habits—participate in the training he needs? At some points, to repeat, parents who care for their children and for the safety of others, cannot allow certain patterns of action (such as running across the street at will, or indiscriminatingly throwing stones). Furthermore, when the child cannot possibly understand or anticipate the consequences of his own behavior, the parent must accept the responsibility for the child's action. But does the parent who cares for the child's development not try as soon as possible, and as much as possible, to reason with the child and show him why these precautions are to be taken? In sum, must the parent who loves his child not try to understand how the child, with *his* nature, can best participate in the guidance of *his* own action in a way to increase the good and prevent unnecessary harm?

We have been outlining the basic predicament which every parent and child faces in order to make clear two meanings of "good" and "love" which are frequently confused. What we mean by a "good" parent and what we mean by "love" in this parent-child relation depends on whether we think that a parent is being good to his child if he does not allow that child, within limits, to take part in the decisions which affect even his own health.

Must love not protect freedom?

I am assuming that a loving parent and a good parent desires the good of the child. And I am asking: Can we, then, believe that a parent loves his child if he is concerned only about his, the parent's security, or only about the security of others, with the result that the child has no share in deciding about actions involving him which he can understand? Does love for child mean that the child must be made to feel dependent upon the parent for safety even when, probably, much of that safety could be left in the child's own hands? Does being "good" to a child mean making sure that he will always do the approved thing whether *he* approves or not?

Everyone must make his choice here, and I must state

my own and try to defend it as preferable to the alternative. I cannot accept a definition of either love or goodness, in terms of obedience at the expense of creativity, or even in terms of safety for all at the expense of freedom. *To be good to, or to love, a human being cannot mean safety for any of us at the cost of freedom and creativity.* One might love an animal, or an infant, before he has any ability to anticipate the future or learn from the past, by providing for safety only. But here freedom and creativity are not lost, for there is none to be lost. The moment any being can be self-conscious enough to know what is happening to him, and the moment he begins to be able to apply his experience for the sake of new experiences, it becomes my duty, as I understand love, and as I understand goodness, to help *him* to understand to the utmost of my ability and of his capacity, what it means to be a self-conscious being who can help and hurt himself and others.

We must pause to draw out some implications of accepting this meaning of *goodness* and *love* toward another. I am parting intellectual company with anyone who says that when we are dealing with persons who can be aware of some (at least) of their motives, or when we are dealing with persons who understand some (at least) of the consequences of their actions, it would be an act of goodness and of love on our part, to encourage them to do only what *we* thought was good for them and for us. I am not blinking at an important fact. Many of our human relations are complicated by the very fact that we differ with each other about what is right for us. And I do not deny that each of us has an obligation to do his best to prevent others, who act in accordance with their conception of goodness, from enacting laws which go against our own convictions about what is good. Yet, which of us, on reflection, would prefer to have agreement at the expense of freedom to stand for our convictions? We are forced, once more, to ask which values we put first.

What, in short, is the pearl of great price, for which, if we had to, we would sell, or *should* sell, all our other jewels? It may be obvious to the reader now that I would choose *creativity* as the experience which I treasure for all of u's. Where there is no respect for creativity there is no lasting goodness. There is no love where there is no creativity or respect for creativity. This means that no matter how safe I think I am making a human being, I am not making him safe *as a human being,* unless I (and he) make it safe for him to be creative! For me to love a person is to do everything in my power to encourage him to be creative! To love him is to risk, if need be, some goods for the sake of greater goods; to love him is to risk them myself, and to allow him to risk them for the sake of growth. More must be said, as we move on, to define more adequately what creativity involves, but nothing will be said to contradict what seems to me to be a great paradox of life—that to be creative means to be free to take risks; to be creative means to be free not to be safe. Yet to be *safe* and to *stay* at the top of my humanity I must respect creativity *in* myself and in others.

Could God be good and not allow creativity?

Can we now go on to say that *if we reason from our experience,* there would be no meaning to talking about a good God if that God could grant man creativity but did not? Later we shall have more to say about whether God can be held to our best human standards. But now I shall simply say that if we are to use the word "good" for God in any sense that can have meaning for human beings, we must be able to point to something in human experience that God's goodness resembles to some extent.[2]

[2] The question of the grounds for attributing goodness to God is discussed more extensively in my *Introduction to Philosophy of Religion* and in a manner more directly connected with this book in "Can the Goodness of God Be Empirically Grounded," in *The Journal of Bible and Religion,* 25 (April, 1957), pp. 99-105.

Let me be more specific. I am saying that so far as I can see, goodness toward man means allowing him to be creative. And any being, God or man, who sponsors creativity must risk "man's inhumanity to man." In creating man *for creativity* God conferred upon man, *so far as human experience testifies,* the noblest of goods. Indeed, as I see it, the very meaning of God's love for man consists in his having allowed men, within their limits, to participate in their own development. But because so much evil has occurred owing to the use and abuse of human creativity, because in our own day we may use our creative ability to annihilate each other through nuclear and bacterial warfare, we must continue to ask ourselves carefully whether creativity is in fact worth it.

When I ask myself why creativity is so essential to goodness and love, I find that I cannot escape three interrelated facts of life: First, that no other good in human life is as good as it might be, if it is not pervaded with, or related to, creativity. Second, that without creativity we actually lose other goods. Third, that creativity, though it involves risks to all concerned, is less of a risk for human beings than any other value or good we prize. It is this assertion, that no other good in life is as good as it might be without creativity, that each of us must justify by looking into his own experience. It may help us to understand our experience, if we examine the problem most of us have with our experience of love.

IS IT ENOUGH TO BE LOVED?

It is probable that when most of us think of love we think of being loved. The theme song in our lives, from infancy on, has been "I want to be loved." Love has meant approval, affection, security; and the younger we were, the more important it was to gain love. The fact that we begin life in complete dependence upon the care of others, the fact that in our earliest days we want and need more than we can get with our own abilities, soon creates in us a yearning for security which we translate into the hunger for love. We learn all too soon that when others are affectionate toward us we can "wangle" things so that we get what we think we need. And before we realize it, we are already at the point where we not only need love, but *demand* it! That is, we now want love not simply because we like affection, but because we can use it as a means of ensuring our getting what we want when we want it.

The more we were allowed by those who "loved" us to *use them* to get what *we wanted* (even though we could have gotten it ourselves), the more have we found ourselves afraid to lose such "convenient" love; for as we grew older we still had these want-habits, but, alas, no confidence in our own capacity to gratify them. In other words, this process of "being loved" leaves us with much self-*gratification* but actually little self-*satisfaction*. Life itself, we see, teaches us that our very attempts to use others for gratifying our needs force us to become needlessly dependent upon them. We find our wants growing; yet our abilities to satisfy them have not been trained to grow. In demanding "love" we were asking others to act for us, though we ourselves did little or nothing for ourselves or for them.

In this way, then, love which is interested only in "security" turns out to be insecurity—and insecurity without creativity! We simply cannot take insecurity out of life by putting the emphasis on "being loved," for "being loved" does not call into play our whole natures, and leaves us with a devastating sense of helplessness. Once our whole nature is taken into account, we realize that if each of us is to grow, if each of us is to develop, *there must be insecurity in our lives.* What we actually learn from experience is that the demand for security at the expense of one's own activity in growth does not take us very far in solving the everyday problems each of us faces. To be a person is to need growth, and to grow is to break with the past without knowing exactly what the future will bring.

CAN LOVE BE PRUDENTIAL ONLY?

To be sure, this narrow *prudential love* we have been describing seems better than positive ill will, because it puts the emphasis on "playing it safe." Prudential love does not intend to do harm; it is really based on fear of change and the desire to preserve what is good. But the prudent lover, concerned as he is to save what is good, never acquires the wisdom to see that a person simply cannot stand still. Therefore, he does not see that the problem of life is not so much a matter of preserving good and "keeping everything safe and sound." Life calls for creating new goods. Personality growth demands that we preserve only that part of the present and past which can be used to create the new goods for which each new situation calls.

For example, every sensitive parent is tempted—as a part of his parental responsibility, he may think—to prevent disappointment and sorrow in the life of his child. He "hates" to see his child suffer; it disturbs his own "peace of mind." Perhaps the child will not be able to take the disappointment and sorrow without despair. Perhaps discouragement here may cause other difficult problems in the child's life! Why, then, "take the chance"? Why not prevent the difficulty from arising? Why not wait until the child is a little older and is "better prepared" to take it. The parent may therefore "fix things" so that the child either will not have the disappointment and sorrow, or he may try to take the real edge from them by counterbalancing them somehow. In so doing, by taking more responsibility himself, he has, in fact, avoided personal disturbance though he may feel virtuous for having prevented possible evil.

I would not for a moment be understood to suggest that parents become irresponsible in this attitude toward the problems of growing persons, or that they overlook the possible dangers in allowing children to face situations more difficult than they have the capacity to bear. I consider it basic principle that persons do everything in their power to prevent situations in which children or adults are confronted with more evil than they can bear or turn to good account. But, as the illustration given above may convey, the parent who conceives of his "love" for his child in terms of keeping the child (and himself) "out of danger" is quite likely to underestimate the real possibility of growth in the "dangerous" situation. Instead of asking the question, Why take a chance now? he might well ask, Why not face possible sorrow and disappointment now? Why not let the child develop here and now his capacity for facing—and accepting—insecurity connected with a potential good?

Is it not a fact that parents who would not dream of offense to their children do in fact insult them by lack of faith in their capacity to endure suffering? In most cases children "bounce back" from suffering as rapidly as they do from physical illnesses—and especially when there is a sympathetic and encouraging parent at hand to help. The "prudent" parent, confronted with the problem of whether to encourage the youngster to do something which may bring more grief than he realized, is more likely to emphasize the possible grief than the possible good! Since, actually, he himself fears suffering more than he cares to create good, he will prefer to put off the test. In so doing, however, he may well be keeping the child from developing the self-confidence that comes from knowing that he can accomplish uncertain objectives—or from knowing that he can take disappointment!

There is another ground for putting more accent on creativity than on prudential love. Much human disappointment and sorrow depends less on the objective situation than on the individual's "level of expectancy." It is the level of expectancy that determines the "level of frustration." The person used to "success," the person who takes comfort and security as a matter of course, begins to suffer frustration the moment things begin to go wrong. It is pathetic, for example, to see human beings, who are fairly well off in every good that others can bestow upon them, feel so insecure because they hardly know what they would do "if something goes wrong." The cause for much groundless disappointment and sorrow is often nothing more than the person's own fear of insecurity. He fears that he cannot stand suffering, and this fear creates his situation of insecurity and frustration.

To summarize: prudential love, love which emphasizes safety, is actually not safe! To "play safe" is not to be safe! Prudential love is actually wrong in its calculations, because it does not face all the facts of life. None of us can keep things from changing. Our problem is to analyze change, including physical and mental change, and transform it into growth, into creativity. And to do this we must move from prudential love into creative love—that is, the love which lives in changing situations, accepts the facts in every situation, but does its utmost to transform the total situation into one in which persons will have another kind of security, the security of growing fellowship or community.

THE NEED IS TO LOVE, NOT TO BE LOVED.

The meaning of creative love is by no means easy to define, since there is no formula for it. It is not correct even to oppose it to prudential love, as if it were not concerned with the preservation of the person. It is rather guided by a different, more inclusive ideal of what the good life for a person is.

Let me repeat that our conception of the nature of a good life is often shaped by our experiences as children in which safety is a necessity. Furthermore, since the dependence of children upon parents is necessarily so great, it is all too easy for any child to grow up demanding love as a basis for his security. This very dependence brings forth as the theme of life: I want *to be* loved. That an infant and a growing child need love is, of course, not to be deplored. Nor should the child's need to be loved be denied, for it springs from his inner nature, as well as from the uncertainty he fears when love is denied, or supplanted by indifference or hostility.

But our question is, Should the need "to be loved" be allowed to dominate the conception of what makes life good? If the love that is showered upon children is one which simply caters to their wants for comfort, or if the love is given on the condition that the parent's demands be acceded to in slavish or never-questioning obedience, then the child does develop the conception of love as a prudent self-protective device to be used to manipulate people. I shall never forget the college sophomore who exclaimed: "All the love I have ever known was an emotion used to get control of people."

To generalize: in the human situation, where insecurity is always present, we can understand the use of "love" as a way of achieving security. Much recent psychology has emphasized this "need for love," without pointing out clearly that the need is *to love* as well as *to be loved*.[3] So much has been said about conflict and frustration as a basis for nervous disease and maladjustment that many persons are now more concerned about avoiding conflict and frustration than they are about encouraging frustrations which are in the line of growth. It makes a critical difference whether we think of the happy or good life in terms of love as "security" or as ad-

[3] I am glad to note this more constructive emphasis in the works of G. W. Allport, S. Blanton, Erich Fromm, Paul E. Johnson, A. H. Maslow, Rollo May, A. Montagu, Carl Rogers, and P. Sorokin. See Bibliography at end of this book.

venture in the sharing of life. In fact, there is no more serious maladjustment than that involved in a person's thinking of life only in terms of *being loved,* for now the emphasis is on his own security and satisfaction at all costs. And this, far from bringing security and satisfaction, actually encourages insecurity and dissatisfaction for all concerned. It is therefore sad to see parents denying themselves so that their children will not have to "suffer" as "we did"—implying that they themselves had never been loved enough!

Once again, I am not deploring the spirit of sacrifice for another's good. But I am deploring personal sacrifice which is blind to what seems to me a basic fact about human existence. We can provide basic physical conditions for safety and security, but we cannot ever provide mental security for the person who is unwilling to face, as responsibly as he can, situations which necessarily involve uncertainty and insecurity—simply because they involve him in growth! In such situations the only "creative insecurity" there can be consists, not in the feeling that everything will come out well, but in the conviction that no matter what happens, one can and will fight for the good.

It is hard to put this kind of security, this *quality* of life, into proper words, or to keep it from seeming like the spirit of bitter defiance. But what, in our calm, best moments, do we hope for ourselves when we confront uncertainty and hardship? Is it that we be delivered from this evil, if the alternative be more evil for somebody else? One thinks of the soldier confronted by the morrow's battle. Does he desire to be spared? Of course! But does he not also fervently hope that he will be able to *keep himself in control* during the moments of stress? If he is spared, but has not met his trial valiantly, his relief for his physical safety is spoiled by his realization that he has not won the inner battle of creating the spirit of self-command.

CHARACTER IS THE INNER CORE OF "SECURITY."

To put it sharply: What person feels more "secure" than the person who knows that he will not quail in the midst of danger! What man is freer in spirit than he who knows that suffering alone will not deter him from doing his best in the face of evil? We human beings are, in the last analysis, manacled by our own fear that some evil will happen to us for which we are not prepared. The fool acts as if he could not be overcome by evil; the coward will give up every other good thing he has if only he can be spared evil; the mature man is never free from danger but is confident that he will not cringe in panic even before an evil which may destroy him. The mature man does not see his life only in terms of what can happen to him, but also, and mainly, in terms of whether he can maintain his ideals. The meaning of his life comes home to him as the creative effort to live up to his ideals without flinching.

Again, we know in the last analysis that our characters are the one thing we can and must create for ourselves. What is our character? It is our will to live by our ideals, "sacrificing" whatever is needed to realize them ever more completely. And we know that our character is the fortress that we must build by our own efforts, since every stone in it must be lifted out of our own thoughts and desires, carefully selected by each of us, and kept in place by our own wills under the stress of siege.

I know that there are those who will feel as they read these last pages that I simply do not understand, in my "liberal" optimism, the real dynamics of life. There will be the psychoanalysts and psychologists who would say that I have learned nothing from depth psychologies which should have taught me that the fundamental dynamics of human life work not at such conscious levels of "will" and "reason" but in the unconscious forces. But I certainly do not deny that unconscious factors are present in the situation each person confronts as he strives to fulfill his needs creatively. Yet I insist that every person must ultimately carry on the battle of his life, with whatever insight he can gain, in the conscious vanguard. I do not for a moment disclaim that there are forces in his environment and in his unconscious which can help him to win his battles. This is part of the reason for my "detour" into an analysis of adequate parental love.

Still, however "moralistic" it may seem, the fact is that sooner or later, if a person is to be selective in growth, if he is to choose as well as he can which way "his soul shall go," he must face the insecurity explicit at every critical point of personal growth—such as these considerations: Shall I be kind to someone who does not like me? Shall I work hard for a goal I can realize only several years hence? In all such battles, self-insight and a permissive unconscious will help tremendously. But is there any more pathetic fact, in our times, than the plight of persons, supposedly enlightened by "dynamic" and "depth" psychology, who think that no creative choice is ever open to them, and that if only they could understand themselves adequately, and then have "emotional blocks" removed, they could enjoy self-actualizing lives?

Curiously enough, I would probably also be accused of optimistic and austere "moralism" by some Christian thinkers of fundamentalist, existentialist, and neo-orthodox persuasion. If depth psychologists would be concerned by my seeming neglect of the unconscious, these thinkers would say that I have too much faith in man's ability to "pull himself up by his own bootstraps." In a word, I have overlooked the need for God as revealed in Christ and the dependence of the human being "on Him" for redemption and strength. Later I hope to say more about this, but here I would want to say that if it be "moralistic" to emphasize human freedom and creativity, then I am indeed moralistic. In any case, if our analysis is correct, it would seem to be God's will that we accept our freedom and use it creatively. However, to emphasize creativity is not to deny human dependence upon God, but to praise God for creativity rather than for security! The creative person is certainly no less dependent upon God than he is upon his unconscious or his human environment. My emphasis would be on what God and man can do *together*.

I would not be misunderstood. There are other things in life that are precious, such as health and knowledge, beauty, fellowship with God, and the joy of loving—without them life would lose much of its savor. But we know that all of them depend to some extent upon good fortune. The one thing that depends upon us alone, and the one thing which undergirds the other blessings, is our unflinching and constant determination to develop these other values despite the insecurities that surround them.

Must Not a Good God Create and Support Creativity?

It may now be clear why I said that if God had made man so that he could not hurt himself or others, man would not be a morally mature person. What makes life most meaningful is not the security provided for us by mother, father, society, or God, but the creative effort which can penetrate into every nook and cranny of our lives. We have seen that for human beings security at the price of creativity means dehumanization. The love for security which forfeits creativity is a snare which turns men into cringing animals and generates a hate of which animals themselves are incapable. If we are to keep the blessings which being human makes possible, we must do so by accepting the risks of being human, and of creatively disciplining ourselves to suffer, whenever need be, for a greater good. It is because we, too much of the time, think that we can preserve our goods by hugging them to ourselves, it is because we conceive even of love as guaranteeing serenity, that we are in fact inhuman to ourselves and to each other. Persons who are not willing to help each other to be creative, persons who are suspicious of the creativity which seems to endanger their present good, live by putting up barricades between people, and they do all in their power to weaken the creative urge in others. But when persons live in a way that seeks to protect the freedom and creativity of others as much as possible, they find new reaches of goodness in their lives, and do not increase the insecurity of life foolishly.

Nor is the reply complete to the person claiming that a God who values for man such creative adventure is a fool. We certainly must not deny the awful reality of the evil men do to each other. We cannot minimize either the cheap little tricks which men play on each other or the wholesale frauds by which they cheat each other. We shall not belittle the frightful toll which fear, hostility, and aggressive feelings take every day in anxiety and nervous tension. We shall rather urge that men are in fact cruel to each other largely because they misconceive the conditions of their own deepest satisfactions. It is their exclusive demand to be loved, to be secure that keeps men tense and uses up their energy without actually providing the only security open to them as men. They do not see that the condition of human security is creative insecurity. They never see that creativity does not endanger the other blessings of life overmuch. After all, creativity creates other values, otherwise it would become pointless. But there is no value more significant than creativity itself—that is, the freedom to use one's own abilities to help bring into being what one believes to be good.

If this be granted, we repeat that any Being who would be good to man would endow man with as much creativity as would be desirable in the kind of world he inhabits. He would not be deterred from granting man creativity because man might abuse it and cut down his own creativity and that of others. If we believe that freedom to create within limits is the pearl of great price, we would morally condemn any person, finite or infinite, who would choose some other goal than freedom to create. In a word, if I were to be as blunt as my student was, I would say, "Any God who rejects creative freedom for the sake of other values, is a fool."

Creativity Demands Dependability

There is, however, another aspect of creativity not stressed in our discussion. The simplest observation of daily life will serve to bring out the fact that our freedom and creativity are always tied in with some regularity. Indeed, if we could not expect regularity, our creativity would be worthless, and we would not exercise it. If the pen I moved across the page did not move in accordance with my will and with what I have learned in the past to expect from fountain pens, ink, and paper I would soon give up the attempt to write. I choose to use my fountain pen because I want the uninterrupted flow of writing and the stability of script which from past performance I know it will give me. But the moment I choose the pen, I am free to write only with pen properties. If I choose pencil, I am restricted to other properties. Any choice I make is a choice which develops me in the act of choosing but restricts me to some sort of regularity. I would not know what to do otherwise; and would remain immobilized until I could anticipate some conclusion to my creative action. I would, for example, be discouraged from developing the habit of kindness or honesty if I felt that I would be just as tempted to be dishonest after years of effort as I would had I not developed the habit in the past. *To be free to create is to choose which regularity one wishes to take advantage of, which regularity to create.*

If this is true, then whether God chooses to create or whether man chooses to create, creation can achieve anything only by using stability for its purpose. Any creative agent preserves any specific creation only by sustaining regularity in that creation. To go even a step further, we cannot know what creativity can actually achieve unless what is created does endure and does make a noticeable difference to other things. We cannot, then, escape from the fact that creativity must work within "poles." At one pole, creativity destroys itself if it is tied forever to only one channel and one rigid manner of acting. At the other pole, freedom or creativity can do nothing worthwhile unless it creates the dependable.

One other example may help us to see concretely the paradoxical way in which the creativity in our lives must always risk itself in the very act of using regular means to express itself. A person who drives a high-powered automobile can achieve speed and distance with greater comfort than one who is limited to an average car. But both persons achieve freedom in space by restricting themselves to the laws of their vehicles and each pays a different price for his achievement. They conquer space by allowing themselves to be controlled by the physical energy whch governs their automobiles. The heavier car that gives more road-comfort makes demands other cars do not make, and anyone who has elected to drive such a car elects to be conformed to its action. He gains the freedom it gives him by accepting all the risks that it exposes him to, and he cannot accept one part of the mechanism without accepting the other.

We turn, once more, to what it means for God to endow man with creativity. If God was to allow man creativity, He had to involve it within the stable structure of man's capacities, and within a world of order which man could understand and use for purposes of creativity. But, to protect creativity, the same man who can understand the laws of nature enough to contrive machines must also be allowed to use them to destroy life. The man who can understand the cause-and-effect relationships governing the human body and mind has to be allowed the freedom to torture the minds and bodies of men. Furthermore, God himself has to live with the man he has made, and with all the consequences of the "cars" which express man's creative use of his endowments. Both the purposes of God and of man are affected by man's use of his creativity. God is the creator of co-creators, for man does not create outright—that is, the very possibilities of creation. But man is co-creator with God; and God is implicated in the creations, the good and the bad creation of man. Likewise, man as co-creator with God has to accept the consequences of the order within which God must work if man's creativity is to exist at all.

Our total discussion, accordingly, moves to the conclusion that to call God good is to say that God created persons whose creativity was a crucial consideration. Any creativity, in turn, would be limited within, but not bounded by, regularities in man's nature and in the world about him. Man, above all, could demand to love or to be loved (or both); and either choice would release certain effects in his own nature and in that of others. God and man both would have to begin where these consequences made their impact. The human father, we have suggested, does not, at his best, seek security at the expense of the creativity which is basic to every profound human satisfaction. The divine Father, in respect for human creativity, accepts many consequences which he himself would not will, but which cannot be avoided when they follow from human volition. In God's willingness to do all in his power to help men develop their creativity, we find the supreme nature of the Love which we begin to know when we too love creativity more than security.

Finally, whatever else we may believe about Christian doctrine, whatever else we may think about the nature of Jesus and of his relation to God, it seems to me that there is a core of meaning in his death upon the cross which we cannot escape, and which is crucial, I believe, to Christian thinking. That meaning goes beyond even the realization that both God and man suffer when men in their moral confusion and self-righteousness crucify the innocent. The Cross forces us to the new, pregnant awareness that to be divine is to accept as creatively as possible full responsibility for, and the consequences of, human freedom. The Jesus who in the wilderness, before beginning his ministry, refused the beguiling securities offered by Satan, the "son of man" who, having "no place to lay his head," yet could see and serve God in fisherman, tax collector, and prostitute—this was the kind of being who *could* "endure the shame" of the cross with a spirit which gives new poignancy to the poor words, "creative insecurity."

Religion as Creative Insecurity

Creativity, we have said, is a basic constituent in man's nature. God, we have suggested, could have expressed his love for man in no better way than to endow him with the capacity to recreate his own nature within the flexible bounds of his abilities. This allowance on God's part involved far-reaching, calculated risks, for, in so doing, God made it possible for man to destroy many of the possibilities for goodness in the world. Men could now let loose upon each other suffering and evil not in accord with God's own will. Yet if the productive moments in man's experience are his highest moments, can we be clear at all about God's purposes for man without trying to understand what this fact of creativity means for our relationship to Him and to each other?

One thing certainly is evident. God did not conceive the good for man as a gift to be given man in one package, as it were, indestructible by anything man could do. Human life is not built like a mechanical model of some sort, put together once for all by God. Nor is it a magnificent work of art by God, expressive of his nature alone. A person is, from embryo to grave, a changing being, with his own destiny and that of others involved at every point in the process.

In this chapter and the final one, we must explore further what the presence of creativity involves for the development of persons and for the relation of persons to God.

What It Means to Be Human

As human beings, we inherit basic human capacities and urges which work in us and ultimately control the extent to which we can develop. But, again, our capacities are not given "in a lump," as it were, "once for all." And neither needs nor capacities go on and off in all-or-none fashion, as electric bulbs do. Nor do we know how far we can go with them. Whatever the limits of our capacities, each of us knows that within these limits, it is "up to me." That is, it is always an expression of my creativity as to how my capacities and urges shall participate in the structure that becomes my personality. Of course the environment affects us, but to what extent does the particular way in which it influences us depend on what we do in responding to its nature? It is true that we live in an environment; but it is even truer to say that each of us lives in "his own environment," the one he has selected from the possibilities offered in the larger world. Our creativity determines within limits what we shall do with ourselves and with our environments to produce the specific character and personality we have in the environment we have made our own.

How little aware we usually are of how much depends on our own effort, comes out when we realize that there is no utter compulsion, for example, that keeps us from doing away with ourselves. Yet how often we find ourselves preferring almost anything to death! But even our death can be our last creative act! We have all assumed so much that a "man does not want to die" that we have made the "will to live" the fundamental drive of life. But strongly as this "will to live" may assert itself, we are not, like animals, unreflective beings who cannot stop to ask ourselves where we are going, why we are living, and whether this kind of life is worth while. I suspect that each of us, at some time in the past, *made up his mind* that he must live as long as he could. Even though it may be impossible for us to date such a decision, it is this basic creative *decision* to live—the *will* to live, indeed, not just the urge to live—which forms the usually unchallenged background of the other decisions we make.

I am not trying to belittle the power of a psychic and biological urge which we may well take for granted. But I am protesting the assumption that seems to me to be hidden in such expressions as this: Man, like animal, has the urge to live. To be human does not mean that another layer has been added to the foundation of animal passion. We cannot assume that in man a "blind" urge to live explains the persistent adjustments for survival, as it may in animal life, because, in so doing, we overlook the fact that man, whatever his anatomical similarities to animal, is a psychic being in whom the urges of animals are transformed.

At any rate, so great are the differences between animal and human needs that we blind ourselves to unique human potentialities when we think of man as a set of complicated variations on an animal pattern.[1] For our purposes here, we must realize that the urge to live is not unquestioned in human life. A man is an underdeveloped man until that urge to live does indeed become the choice to live—that is, the will to live for this and not for that. In other words, it is the *decision to live or not to live* which raises man above the animal. This decision a man probably makes in the midst of suffering and uncertainty—it may be at some time in childhood when disappointment is keen. In this decision a man *reaffirms* reflectively the urge to live and chooses among

[1] See Chapters One, Two, and Four in my *Free Will, Responsibility, and Grace* (New York: Abingdon Press, 1957).

alternative directions open to him.[2] The purpose of life, as Socrates so well put it, is not to live, but to live well; and, he added, the unexamined life is not worth living!

Again, I am not concerned to give a complete account of the genesis of such a decision in the growth of a person, and I am not suggesting that it takes the dramatic, direct form: "To be or not to be, That is the question." But I am concerned to protest the conception of a man's life in which he is seen as another animal dominated by an unquestioning, blind urge, which, far from involving a creative decision, uses everything at his disposal simply as a means for getting his own satisfaction. A man questions his "urge to live" and its various ways to satisfaction. A man can put himself to death. (As a matter of fact, most of us do kill ourselves, but not all at once! We kill the man in us in little convenient doses which keep us from being much more than higher animals!) A man becomes some *sort of man*. He creates some specific form of existence, the moment he *decides* to live for something.

The first creative act in our lives, then, is to will to live, despite pain and inconvenience. This is not the place to discuss any philosophy of life which, like the Buddhist, maintains that the goal of life is to cease from willing. But even the suggestion that peace comes only as we give up "the will to live" indicates that man must make a choice about the

[2] I am glad to find a similar emphasis on creativity in the work of Paul Tillich, generally and especially in *The Courage to Be* (New Haven, Conn.: Yale University Press, 1952) and *Dynamics of Faith* (New York: Harper, 1957). But there are underlying differences within broad agreements, in theory of knowledge and world view in Professor Tillich's thought which lead to a different interpretation of what creativity involves in man and in his relation to God. The main text of my *Religion as Creative Insecurity* was drafted before I got the opportunity to read *The Courage to Be*, and it was finished before the publication of Erich Fromm's *The Art of Loving*. Readers of this book owe it to themselves to study these books for different final interpretations of faith, love, and creativity. See footnote later, p. 101.

hold which the urge to live shall have over him. Creativity is the essence of any survival in which a human being is implicated. Man is born in uncertainty and insecurity. From the beginning of his *reasoning* existence as a human being, he must be creative to some degree, or sink below the animal!

Why do we repeat our theme again and again? Why do we emphasize that within each changing, growing person there comes that point in his development where he knows that he must take his own risk in determining for which possibilities in his own life (and in all about him in so far as it depends on him), he will "vote"? The answer is, Because we have been told from many sides that man must be seen in the light of his evolutionary origins, that he is an intricate set of built-in mechanisms which are responsible for his survival, that there are deep, subterranean, unconscious forces with which he must deal, that he must "adjust" these forces to the environment. We have been told that we must not glorify man's reason as a guide in living, that about all man's reason can do is to keep his powerful, unconscious drives from destroying him as he does his best to keep the peace of mind and security he treasures above all else.

There is enough truth in all these and similar contentions to allow a half-true misconception of what man's essential nature is. Man, we contend, is a creator. But we also stress that he creates within bounds. As creator he does not exceed the limits of the laws which describe physical, biological, and psychological events. But he does choose which cause-and-effect sequences he will use as a basis for the future. We have emphasized the fact that creativity, in order to create anything specific, must create some stable regularity. To create something that is anything at all is to create something which can be trusted to have some kind of effect upon other things, including the creator. Thus, any creator, whether God or man, is bound by this inexorable law. God and man have their respective kinds of power and creativity, but what they create, once created, has a nature which has certain effects and not others. This means that what is created will have a restrictive effect upon other beings and upon the creator.

Again, creativity is fundamental, but it is not the whole story. It does not create the laws of physics, biology, or psychology which it uses. But neither does it create "all by itself" and "at will" the values and ideals by which it guides itself. Physical and biological laws are already "there," and we are tempted to think that we ourselves make up the moral "laws" and ideals by which we guide our action. In what follows we shall see that we cannot create as we please in the moral and spiritual areas of life if we would get the most out of our human potentialities. We shall, therefore, ask: What direction can human creativity take in order to produce the conditions that will not in the future make creativity more difficult?

Conditions of Creativity

In our last chapter, in developing the meaning of love, we urged that much damage to creativity might be done if love degenerated into shortsighted prudence. As we saw, parents who focus on protecting the child from being hurt or disappointed may well be encouraging the child to think of life in terms of "saving myself trouble." The youngster subjected to such "protecting love" may learn too well to avoid situations in which he feels insecure. As a result, the child does not learn that he can take a great deal of disappointment, or how to "take it." What is more, he does not get done the things which he probably could do. On the other hand, a difficult, insecure situation which he learned to manage successfully would provide balm for hurt feelings, refreshment for fatigue, and a backlog of "accomplishment" for facing future insecurity with confidence.

It should be clear, then, that the development of positive creativity requires the most circumspect study of our capacities as human beings. The desire to become creative can unleash disappointment and despair; it can give birth to anxiety and bitterness. The person disappointed in the attempt to be creative can come to have more faith in power than in mercy and justice; he can be overcome by that cynicism which stems from distrust of others. Indeed, when the easy turn to destructiveness, which can spring from the creative urge, is overlooked, we develop that "cult of creativity" which confuses creativity with an uncritical self-expression. Then creativity is conceived, falsely, as the opposite of restraint. But the creative life is not opposed to discipline, and it is not a flight from control. It transforms fear into positive caution; it opposes self-indulgence, even as it attempts to face insecurity with some plan of action.

Neglect of these considerations is seen quite clearly, once more, when parents who misunderstood the requirements for creativity have thought they were encouraging their children to be creative when they allowed them to do what they wanted. They made sure not to "impose" unwanted tasks on their children, and to avoid unwanted or "awkward" social situations. But the child who is allowed to do "what he wants" may begin to view the world only in the light of his wants. As a result, his creativity may turn to gratifying wants. He tends to view others in relation solely to his desires, or their ability to help him gratify himself. He may "get along" very well as long as his permissive parents and indulgent family and friends conform themselves to his wants, and put their abilities at the disposal of his claims upon them. But whether he or his parents like it or not, his wants are only one part of his nature. Wants have to be related to physical and intellectual and emotional capacity (as well as the environmental possibilities).

Because no person can always depend upon the ability of

others to get him what he wants, and because his own ability not only has limitations but will be limited by the wants and abilities of others, the attitude a person takes toward his own wants is vital to the way in which he will be creative. I am not saying what is so frequently said: "The sooner one learns that he cannot get all he wants, the better." The critical point in creativity is not whether or not one gets what he wants, but whether he realizes first that his wants—not to be despised—are to be fulfilled through his own abilities. It is easy to want, and no sooner does a growing person become self-conscious than he realizes increasingly what he wants. But the turn his creativity will take depends (not once and for all to be sure) on whether he budgets his wants against his ability to satisfy them. Whether he likes to or not, he needs to learn to correlate wants and abilities; for, as we have said, even assuming that others would always cater to his desires, human experience teaches that others cannot always do for him what he alone can do for himself. Much of the art of life is not that of getting other people to do things for one—much as this is what developing a "personality" is frequently thought to mean—but in learning how to develop abilities so that wants can be satisfied. When this is not possible (either owing to one's inability or to an uncooperative environment), the problem is to prune wants to meet abilities. The child who learns to live on credit will have to learn the hard way that life has a way of increasing the payments of interest in proportion to the risk it finds the debtor to be.

Creativity, then, is protected and enhanced by careful and circumspect planning. Far from being opposed to restraint, it builds in and through it. The problem is to realize that because human life operates within human potentialities and human limitations, and because one cannot always live in the environment immediately suited to his wants and abilities, it is important to focus on matching and mating abilities not only with one's own needs and wants but also with the wants, needs, and abilities of others. No one knows ahead of time, and the inexperienced person least of all, how well his own integration of wants and abilities can be effected. The temptation is great to give up and "leave well enough alone," and to depend upon adjustments already made by others, by "playing up" to them. One may thus try to escape the insecurity which must be part of any creative, adaptive process.

It is for this reason that the nurture of creativity calls for special qualities in those upon whom the person feels dependent. The growing child, especially, needs to feel that what he does will not seriously risk the approval of his parents. For them to be "long-suffering" and "patient" is important, but this is a halfway house. If they encourage him positively to find his own best way out of problems as they come along, he will realize that he must judge his efforts not by conformity alone, but by promise of further growth. Crucial will be their attitude toward his failure. If he feels that they have faith in him, if he knows that they are willing to share his failures as well as his successes, he will be encouraged to face the possibility of disappointment and failure that may have to be his. Over and over again, individuals refuse to discover the truth about their abilities because they fear that others will make them suffer for their deficits in ability, or for their failures. Each of us is more likely to venture into new pathways if he feels that there are those who will stand by him when the voyage of discovering ends in failure.

If these observations are true, can we not affirm what we might well call "the Law of Creativity": *Creativity becomes fertile when each person takes the responsibility for it, both in himself and in others*? That is, creativity will be directed in each person not into building defenses against the impositions and demands of others, and not into raising self-protective mechanisms which focus attention on immediate "peace of mind." Creativity will be directed toward accepting failures as part of the process of understanding and living with others. The more of our thought, time, and effort we can shift from defense against failure to the positive planning and realizing of ventures in self-creation, the more life will mean to us. But in our self-creation we cannot be indifferent to the need that others have for our loyalty to them as they attempt to re-create themselves. If we care only for our own productivity, we shall be forced, by processes beyond our control, to spend more time, energy, and thought, on our fears!

All of which is another way of stating the basis for our earlier theme: Creativity needs love, and love worthy of the name is love of productive creativity. In our last chapter we emphasized the importance of the transition from the immature, childish want *for* love, to the maturer need *to* love. Until a human being moves from the weak, parasitic state of being loved to the co-operative state of wanting to love, he does not know the difference between gratification and satisfaction. We have stressed the need that children have for parents who will encourage them to find themselves and stand by them sympathetically and loyally when failure occurs. Obviously this cannot happen if persons stay in the childish stage of wanting to be loved instead of loving.

The Effects of Positive Creativity

At this point some reader may ask: But isn't your concept of creativity still too vague to be any guide in action? You seem to insist that positive creativity is not a catering to want and desire as such. You urge that wants be harmonized with abilities. You stress that persons must feel confident that others will not take advantage of their failures. But once we leave homely illustrations of parent-child interaction, what does productive creativity involve in adult relationships?

The answer, of course, must be that only a fully developed ethics—much more than is being attempted here—would begin to satisfy this demand. But the implications of our theme for two critical areas of tension between persons can now be examined.

In the first place, productive creativity would, I believe, lead to growth in self-respect; that is, respect for one's own wants and abilities, and for his responsibility to harmonize them as well as possible. Indeed, to respect either oneself or another person is to respect the possibility of growth. Here an area of conflict and tension immediately develops between persons whose wants and abilities differ, and whose goals conflict. What does productive creativity require when equally conscientious persons find themselves actually working toward goals that conflict with, or directly contradict, each other?

Very serious problems come up here, but basic, it seems to me, is the obligation to respect not only the growth of creativity in oneself but its growth in others. This means that as a matter of policy, one ought never to use another's creativity simply as a means to his own ends. *The focus is not so much on doing certain things, no matter how good, but on maintaining an emotional and moral climate in which people will always feel encouraged to express their considered opinion on any problem confronting them as persons in a society of persons.*

We are here actually defining the meaning of creative tolerance. Tolerance is the willingness to bear with, to suffer with, the person who honestly disagrees even with one's own most cherished convictions. It is not simply a favor granted by one man to others. It is what cements persons together even as they differ. It is a socializing necessity, for it calls each person to listen to what his opponent is saying. It leaves open the avenues for conversation and for every honest effort to persuade each other of the truth on the matter at issue. As loyal love is the need of the growing child in his search for himself, so tolerance is what any human being needs from the very people who think he is wrong.

But here the person receiving the tolerance must also remember that he cannot expect those who tolerate him to act as if they agreed with him! A Democrat tolerates a Republican as they seek to discuss an issue, but if he cannot agree with the Republican on the given issue, he votes against him. Each of us must realize, if he is in the minority, that those who do not agree with our views, once having protected our freedom to voice our objections, must demand obedience to legislation until such time as we, through persuasion, can procure the repeal of that legislation. It is not easy for one side of a dispute to see another side win, but once the door is left open for further discussion and persuasion, the majority has a right to expect that what it believes to be the best alternative be respected in action.

Tolerance, then, like creativity, cannot live where there is no conformity. Nor can it live where there is no opportunity to be "wrong" or "out of step." And tolerance, as a servant of productive creativity, will not expect people to deal lightly with the actions and words which they believe threaten their own goals for creativity. Tolerance involves the insistence that we be heard, but we must be willing to suffer for not being able to persuade the majority; we must learn to be "outsiders" for the sake of our convictions. In a word, the minority can demand no *privileged* position in the name of tolerance. It must expect to sacrifice for its convictions as part of its tribute to the sincere convictions of others, who, consistently, must punish those who break the rules of the game of tolerance. The plea for tolerance must go hand in hand with the willingness to suffer defeat for one's minority opinion, and with the willingness to co-operate in action, though not in verdict, once the will of the majority is clear.[3]

Creativity as Forgiving Love

This discussion of tolerance brings us to a second, even more crucial area of conflict, the area in which persons must deal with those who have purposely failed to honor their personal and social obligations—the area of forgiving love. Forgiveness is in fact the highest expression of love, and the best encouragement for creativity. It demands real insight into the predicament which human beings, born in freedom, face.

As we have seen, freedom and creativity involve the real possibility and probability that human beings will hurt each other, not only unwillingly, but purposely. The person who, far from forgiving, has used his creativity consciously to deprive another of what belongs to him, the person who acts as if the world and other persons were simply his to be used as he pleases, the person who thinks of other persons as forces to be mastered and subjugated to his own ends, that person is a tyrant in the making—though actually he is allowing his passions to tyrannize over him. He is the conscious foe of every person who is trying to be a freer person through the fuller development of his own powers. He is suspicious of every action which might decrease his feeling of security. He ends up being feared and despised—when he cannot be overwhelmed—by those who feel too weak to challenge his power. He frightens those who feel the impulse to like him, since they fear that he will use their benevolent feeling for his own purposes. At the same time, he is himself so suspicious of others that he cannot "take any chances." He cannot forgive those who hurt him even accidentally, since

[3] This emphasis does not foreclose the possibility that a person, like Socrates or Jesus, may believe an issue so important that he would rather die resisting the majority verdict than conform.

he is afraid that others will take advantage of his "good nature."

In short, the trouble with distrust is that it breeds distrust both in him who has it and in him toward whom it is directed. Both distruster and distrusted suffer. Everyone suffers where forgiveness is not allowed to ease the tension when human beings hurt each other. When the possibility of forgiveness is eliminated by narrow egotism and distrust, the situation is ripe for uncompromising uncertainty and struggle to the bitter end. If a human being knows that any mistake he makes will be used against him, and if he knows that any error of his which hurts a fellow man will never be forgiven and forgotten, he will not be encouraged to venture into any new path of co-operative action.

The situation of the child (or any dependent) once more throws light on this. The child who fears that his mistakes, even when unintentional, will incur the wrath and revenge of his parents will be strongly tempted always to "let well enough alone," or to hide his mistakes. But if he knows that he can never pass beyond his parents' love and care, that they, however hurt, will do all in their power to help him undo his mistake, or make up for it, or simply live with it (if that is all that can be done)—that child will be encouraged to be creative, and will learn to be cautious but not inhibited.

We have not begun to realize the importance of this psychological fact about human nature. We have blinded ourselves by the aphorism, "To err is human, to forgive divine." What we need to see more clearly is that we are so constructed as human beings that unless we too forgive, we not only shall never approach the divine, but we can never unloose the human potential completely. Human beings who live in fear that they will be judged by the principle, "An eye for an eye and a tooth for a tooth," tend to shrivel up and become mediocre (when worse effects do not occur).

They concentrate on not doing anything bad instead of attempting a greater good. They never break windows, but neither do they light candles.

Only the faith that a possible error will be seen in the light of the desire to improve the total situation will suffice to launch new expeditions into the unknown. No society can thrive without a backlog of good will, or without a generous sense of humor about the evil that men do either out of ignorance or out of well-meant experimentation. The society that concerns itself mainly with catching the evildoer, the society that has more jails than schools, will find itself sooner than later without the keen, adventurous minds it needs to help it meet new problems. Punishment and the threat of punishment may change a behavior pattern, but by themselves, without encouragement to goodness, they produce change without inner growth.

On the other hand, if there is anything that will encourage even habitual evildoers to break their habits, it is confidence that those whom they have hurt will not deal with them only as evildoers but also as persons who can do good. Each of us can refer to his own experience as an evildoer. Have we not been encouraged to confess our misdeeds, to cut them from our lives, by the confidence of others that we could do so? If anything can help an evildoer to follow his own temptation to reform, it is the inspiring power of forgiving love.

In our own day this fact has been illustrated again. One of the strongest factors in the reform of many an alcoholic who has joined Alcoholics Anonymous is the knowledge that his fellows will do all in their power, at any time of night or day, to help him. The prodigal son would probably have gone back to the pigs if his father's attitude had been that of the self-righteous, conventional brother who could not see beyond his own goodness to the need of his brother. Again, whatever be one's final view about the meaning of the Cross in Christian theology, there can be little doubt that when sinful men have believed that God was concerned not with punishing them but with saving them from their sin, they have felt in their lives a force which broke the shackles of their evil ways.

The Re-creation of Confidence by God's Forgiving Love

Some psychologists are inclined to view religion as a sign of immaturity—a desire to return to the snugness of the womb, safely protected from the dangers of existence. That this is true of many "religious" people cannot be doubted by anyone who takes even casual note of the function religion plays in their lives. But this explanation does not begin to account for the mature people who do not want to escape from their problems but are honest enough to realize that they continually miss the mark in their own lives, and hurt others or are insensitive to the hurt in them. Whatever else we human beings have in common, we have sin! We may define specific sins so differently that what one of us regards to be sinful may seem to another morally good. But every man, within the context of his own ideals and aspirations, knows that he has "fallen short," willfully, of the standard he approves; and every man knows what it is to feel unworthy. What is more, each of us faces not only his unworthiness, but also his seeming inability to do anything about it. We feel not only sinful, but trapped in our sin. "If only someone could help me!" "If only I could start over again!" "If only I could break the hold this sin has over me!" In this state of mind, if we can believe that we live in a world in which, whether men care or not, God has not given us up, we feel new hope, and we find within us new springs of energy.

Are we, at such moments, simply running back to a substitute for mother and father? Are we simply seeking for protection? Or are we, in new-born faith, setting out to discover what "re-generation" calls for? Far from returning to the safety of the womb, we are continuing on our journey in the belief that God cares, that he is our comrade in every new effort, thought, and deed. In favor of this interpretation is the testimony of many sensitive and creative religious persons—be it clothed in simple terms or in the richer paraphernalia of theological presentations. In this process of believing and exerting their utmost, they found "new life," not only new strength, but a quality of sober joy which can come only to those who feel accepted despite their sin. Let there be no doubt about it. Such belief that God is not only love, but forgiving love, has generated effort to reform the nature of one's conduct and personality. Anyone who would "pooh-pooh" this kind of motivation prematurely, should remind himself that it is this very motivation that has led many, who seek belief in God, to the couches of psychiatrists.[4] Such persons are usually confronted with thoughts and behavior which they do not approve, let alone understand, and they often feel guilty. Why do they refer their problems to a psychiatrist? Because they are convinced that the psychiatrist will not be concerned to judge them or accuse them. He is anxious to understand the causes for their behavior, and both he and the co-operative patient work together on the assumption that there is power and ability for goodness available, once the blocks are understood and removed. One hardly knows what would result if the patient (and the psychiatrist) could not also hope that friends of the patient would be understanding, and willing, especially during the process of recovery, to forgive and forget aberrations.

Psychopathology, in other words, far from replacing a

[4] I am not suggesting that religious persons should not avail themselves of psychiatric and psychological aid, just as I would not suggest that they ought not to avail themselves of medical or other scientific aids. But all these aids are most effective with persons when there is mutual respect and forgiveness.

motive basic to religion, would get nowhere without it. Indeed, the problem which faces most persons during the process and at the end of the treatment is this: "Now that I understand why I behave in these rigid and undesirable ways, how do I get the strength to change them and not develop other unhealthy modes of life?" Unless the individual can believe in himself, in those around him, in the theory of the doctor as to how his strength will be mustered, he is lost. Different schools of psychotherapy, in devious ways, take us back to the realization that forgiving love is not an idle "theological" doctrine, but the basis of recovery and creativity. And our thesis is that a human being's development and regeneration thrive on the sincere conviction that both man and God, far from being indifferent to him in his weakness and in his sin, do care for him, and that, whatever man does, God's forgiving love joins him in the healing of his wounds as he accepts new responsibilities.

Creativity Developed by Forgiving Love

It would be a curious fact if forgiving love encouraged creativity in the repentant person, but undermined it in the life of the forgiving person. Actually, to be able to forgive is to reach perhaps the highest peak of moral creativity in human experience. The person who can forgive is not only proving that he is a creative person; he is increasing the power and quality of his creativity. Let us see why this is so by contrasting kindness, without which we are hardly human, with forgiveness, without which we can never know the meaning of God in human form.

It requires a certain amount of imagination and power to be kind. The person who cannot lift a finger to help persons or animals who have been hurt is a human being who is himself maimed spiritually. Though few of us begin to be as kind as we ought to be, most of us do not find it difficult to enter sympathetically into the plight of the sick and the crippled. Too often, unfortunately, we do not "follow through" when we feel generous impulses and emotions; nor are we as intelligent as we could be about relieving those who need our help. To be kind is to have strong sympathy, acute imagination, and to act to alleviate the distress of those who are hurt. To be unkind is to suffer from hardening of the emotional arteries, from shrinkage of the imagination, and from impotence of will. To be unkind is to be victimized by our own possessions; for we can give only what we possess, and what does not possess us. To be kind involves the power to reach out and encompass in emotion, in thought, in imagination, the needs of others. Kindness calls for a kind of creative control of ourselves and of our possessions which enables us to serve those needs to the best of our ability.

A person who is unkind, in other words, is strangling in fear and anxiety. He is, as a matter of fact, less than honest with the facts of life. He does not see that all of us live in constant debt to circumstances over which we have no control; nor does he see that many of us have much more than we need or deserve. To claim exclusive ownership of our eyes while the blind are groping and in danger, to claim exclusive ownership of our wealth when the victims of hurricane, flood, and disease have lost all through no fault of their own, means nothing less than dishonesty with the facts of existence. In the presence of the suffering of others, especially when it is caused by factors beyond their control, no honest person can assume that what he can control belongs to him without question—unless he thinks that the world was made for him alone. To shrug one's shoulders and say, "It's his hard luck," is not to face the facts about one's own good luck. A person who develops the habit of facing only those facts which keep him from sharing his goods with others is a slave of his own rigidities and fears; he dares not be grateful for the many goods he has for which he has not worked.

The kind person, on the other hand, not only is honest about the unearned increment of good in his life; he also knows the glow of good-feeling which comes when he does all in his power to keep the hurts another has received from becoming a source of bitterness and loss of faith in his fellow men. The kind person knows all too well that even in sharing the plight of the dispossessed, he is more fortunate than they are. For the hurt and the maimed, even when they are helped, still have to do without something they need. And they must go on facing their necessary dependence on the good will of others. If a kind man knows that he is doing his best to repair the damage of misfortune, he feels a quality of creativity which comes only to those who, knowing gratitude, now realize the full meaning of humility.

But if kindness can be a source of strength in personality, how much more we may expect from forgiveness! The person who is kind, grateful, humble, courageous, is creative in character. But if he can also be forgiving, does he not exemplify the crown trait of moral creativity? Surely there is no more difficult virtue to achieve and carry out effectively.

Forgiveness demands a degree of self-control, and courage, which other virtues, including kindness and meekness, merely begin to approximate. The challenge to forgiveness is one which defies all the rules by which we normally live. "Be kind to those who are hurt? Yes. Be courageous to others who may not appreciate my spirit in giving? Yes. Do everything in my power to help him who has gone out of his way to hurt me purposely? No! This is too much. You are asking me to sustain him who not only cares nothing for me, but who has plotted against me and mine. You are asking me to set up in the business of loving those who have made it their business to destroy heartlessly. You are asking me to strengthen the evil one and to weaken all others who may be hurt by his strength. No!"

It is so easy to be sentimental about forgiveness, or to

appeal to the "heroism" in persons. But no sober estimate of the protestations just cited can afford to be sentimental, for they represent sober reflections of good people, and not the rationalizations of the irresponsible. The facts of life are that most of us do much evil, even as we try to do good, because we are sentimental and act from some momentary emotional impulse, instead of a careful analysis of what is called for as we try to do the good. We must, then, not mimimize the facts to be faced when we, or other persons, are hurt without justification.

Again, forgiveness calls for helping the person who has purposely hurt us when he did not have to do so, or with insufficient provocation. He may have hurt us directly, or he may have endangered the good of the community by wasting his own substance, by getting into needless debt, by playing on all of life's margins for the "thrill of it." But now, here he is, caught in his own trap. Why should we not let him suffer in his trap, and protect ourselves from his further raids on us and the common good? After all, "he asked for it!" Furthermore, what assurance do we have that he would not do the same thing again if we took the sting out of his present situation?

These protests are impressive through their appeal for the preservation of the good we have already achieved and that has now been decreased. And who is not impressed by the power that is added to these protests, when we think of difficulties confronted in forgiving large groups of persons and whole nations, whom we cannot know or judge intimately? Thus, I hardly know where to begin this attempt to show, not that others can profit from our forgiveness, but that our own productive creativity is highest only when we forgive.

Here is a person, let us say, who has purposely hurt me, and without provocation. What must happen to me if I am to forgive him? I am, first of all, to try to understand what factors in his life made it easy for him to do this. Did he misconceive my relation to him, and did I give him any grounds for supposing that I not only did not care for him but, in my self-interest, might be willing to hurt him? To answer these questions will lead me to become perceptive of many facets of human existence and to grow more appreciative of the problems others face. It helps me to develop more insight into the way in which I do things that may be offensive and appear heartless to others. I become vividly aware of the interconnecting links between us as human beings, and cannot overlook the unpurposed disappointment and the tragic consequences of unnecessary deficits in our everyday planning. As I think these things over I become a wiser human being, to say the least.

But if I am to help the culprit, what must I do? I must decide how much to help him to help himself. Do I simply pat him on the back and tell him to "forget it"? Surely this would be adequate for many, many situations. But when the culprit has shown himself capable of serious harm, I am not helping him or anyone else by refusing to hold him responsible for damages done.

I must, therefore, be careful about the end-state which I want any forgiveness to create in such situations. The purpose of forgiveness is not simply to make *me* "feel good." It is for the evildoer to find new confidence in himself, for him to accept all reasonable responsibility for repairing, as far as possible, the damage done. The words, "I shall not exact my pound of flesh from you" do not begin to deal with the problems we both face. For me it is the intricate one of knowing what I can do to co-operate with him, beginning where he is, as he picks himself up with my help, and starts to rebuild his life. I must learn to gauge his despondence and discouragement, and I must convince him of my concern for him. If only I can know when I am expecting too much! If only I can keep him from thinking that I, who might well be in his place, am lording it over him! If I can only help him to be patient while wounds heal or as he reverts to old ways!

For me to begin to recite some of the attitudes and actions which are demanded of me if I am really to forgive, is for me to realize how rich my personality would become as I learned to forgive. What a sense of values, and what depth of compassion I should develop! But what is even more important, I begin to realize that in forgiving him, I am helping to create an atmosphere in which another broken human being may grow without loss of respect for himself.

And now both of us know that when we are willing to forgive each other—how often am I too a sinner!—and give ourselves co-operatively to each other's growth, we have robbed suffering of its sting. *Forgiveness is that quality of creativity in which I lift all I have in careful dedication to the rebuilding of life.* A person cannot create life, but in creative love a human being can help it to flourish; and in creative forgiveness he brings himself to that point of development where the weak can find strength and hope. The wages of sin are death; the wages of forgiveness are creativity.

I am sure that these last few pages—and many other pages —will strike some readers as being much too man-centered and "individualistic" to do justice to the facts of Christian experience; for the emphasis seems to be on what the individual achieves in his own life as he forgives, and what the individual does on his own power. And this seems to deny a fundamental fact of the Christian faith, as many would interpret it. In the Christian view, it will be asserted, man cannot achieve self-sacrificing love of neighbor through his own power but only through the grace of God. The Christian must be as "realistic" as Paul when he confessed that the very things he approved were the ones he found himself unable to do. Only "through Christ who strengtheneth me," did he find it possible to approach the kind of love "which beareth all things."

It is unfortunate, indeed, if I have given the impression that a man can lift himself by his own bootstraps, or that he can achieve the power to forgive without the help of God. How silly it would be to deny that all human beings succumb in some measure to a self-love which turns them from seeing either themselves or others as God wills!

But the question is not so much whether we need God's aid to destroy the chains of self-love, but how we are to conceive of God's aid. It is an undeniable fact of Christian and non-Christian religious experience that a quality of life is possible to those who live in the consciousness of God's love for them and their fellow men, a quality of life which is not otherwise available. I would not dream of denying *the fact* even though I am not satisfied with particular theories about how this happens. I would, however, move with the main tradition in demanding that human freedom of will and human creativity be not abrogated by any theory of Divine grace. No matter how strongly we wish to assert man's need of God in the moral struggle, we destroy the very meaning of the struggle—indeed, the very dignity of human existence which has been accented in these pages—if *at any point* God literally takes control of the human will and changes its course. We cannot with any consistency say that we ourselves turn our wills from God to sin, but that he turns our wills for us when we prodigals turn back to him and his way! In much of the literature on Divine grace the authors would seem to want it both ways.

When most of us speak about doing something "through the grace of God" we do not try to think out exactly what this involves. Nor shall I try here to develop an adequate theory.[5] But just as I would want to insist that God's aid

[5] For a fuller treatment, see Chapter 4 of the author's *Free Will, Responsibility, and Grace* (New York: Abingdon Press, 1957).

to man must not destroy man's own creative freedom, so I would equally insist that man achieves nothing alone. At every moment of his being he is sustained by what he himself does not create. And when he "creates," when he wills, whether he paints a landscape, or builds a bridge, or invites and receives friendship, he is taking advantage of factors already present or potential in himself and his environment. Man, for example, does not become selfish without illustrating certain psychological principles in his own life, and he cannot become unselfish unless he uses resources he himself did not create. We do not always know *how* it is that certain actions of ours make us feel better. Does a lover know much about how it is that his love for his sweetheart changes his life? Yet he says that he would not be what he is without her aid. Does he mean that she changes his will for him? Hardly. It would be closer to the truth to say that the thought of her, of all she means to him, of her love for him, "makes" him want to do his best to be worthy of her by deepening his appreciation of what life can hold in store for those who trust in love.

Similarly, what I have been trying to suggest in these pages is that something happens in the lives of human beings when they adopt a creative attitude of love toward God and toward each other. Let a person take a God of love seriously, let him do all in his power to live in the spirit of God's love, to join God in his concern for all men, and the actual fact of the matter seems to be that he finds a new strength in his life to grow in the struggle against evil as well as in the appreciation of all that makes for good in growth of personalities.

If I am asked, But does man turn his will by himself?, I can only say that to deny this is to deny human freedom and dignity. On the other hand, man does nothing "on his own" except decide in what direction he will "turn" his will, to use an Augustinian word. But once he turns his will he finds the whole world that God has established moving according to God's will and in myriad ways we do not begin to understand. Let a man turn to God with contrite heart and will to accept forgiveness and be forgiving. His very act of trust seems to be part of the conditions for finding the power which he would not otherwise have. Those who have spoken of what they have done "through the grace of God" have been testifying to this fact, even though they may have been expressing it in a way to suggest that God took their lives over. God, it may be suggested, will not "take possession of" a will that does not will to be "his."

The burden of these pages has not been a denial of the need of God, but an attempt to show that we cannot find God adequately, nor he us, unless we adopt an attitude toward him and our fellow men which is the creative insecurity that only lovers and forgivers can know. Far from suggesting that a man lifts himself by his own bootstraps, or that God lifts him by his bootstraps whether or not he adopts a creative attitude of loving trust and concern, I have been insisting that it is in the very midst of our efforts to be creatively insecure toward God and man that we find a power and a blessedness which make the religious life the only one worth living.

To put this differently: What has mankind discovered in its experiments with living? No response to everyday problems or crises is more fruitful, in the last analysis, than facing insecurity creatively. This is the kind of living which moves beyond "being contented" to what I would call the blessedness of creative insecurity. If there is power in such living, it is *not of our own making* but it is of *our own choosing* (within limits established by God's goodness). But what is at stake here is not so much whether man can become forgiving without the help of God, but the very conception of what God's nature is, and what is involved in religious fellowship. And this is the theme of the next chapter.

Religion as Worth-While Suffering

The Warrant for Belief in a Loving Father

The reader may now be clearer about one main purpose of this book. I did not *begin* with the assertion that God is a loving Father who, in his goodness, created free human beings, and whose will it is that men shall live in that creative respect for each other which finds its deepest expression in forgiveness. These convictions, about God and his relation to man, about man and his relations to God and to his fellow man, are central to the Christian interpretation of life. Whatever else we may believe about Jesus, there is no understanding him apart from marking the centrality of these convictions in his thought and action. But I have not maintained that these convictions were true because they were revealed in some direct, infallible, incontrovertible manner by God to man.

Again, I did not appeal to an act of faith to justify belief in these convictions about God and man. This is not because I believe that such "revelation" is unthinkable. The point I would make is that no matter how directly we felt we knew God, no matter how authoritative we thought these experiences were, we would come to distrust them if they were inconsistent with the most reasonable interpretation of the remainder of our experience. As Gordon W. Allport has said, "The developed personality will not fabricate his religion out of some emotional fragment but will seek a theory of Being in which all fragments are meaningfully ordered." [1] Thus, supposing that a person's direct experiences convinced him of God's goodness, would he be entitled to trust this experience unless he could find further evidence of this fact? Even if he did continue to regard his direct experience as trustworthy, he would not convince others of the truth of his conviction. Why, indeed, believe God is good if so much evil is part of human experience? On what other grounds can one justify the Christian teaching that men should love each other to the point of forgiving each other? [2]

It would be our contention that the careful analysis of our actual human experience of goodness is crucial to the justification of belief in God's goodness. And in the last chapter we tried to show that far from being a far-fetched, sentimental view of human life, there simply can be no human fulfillment, no dependable growth, apart from love that moves on to forgiveness. Thus, for example, the psychologist A. H. Maslow supports the findings of an increasing number of psychologists (like Alfred Adler, Karen Horney, Carl Rogers, Erich Fromm, Gordon W. Allport, Harry Stack Sullivan) as well as sociologists and anthropologists (like A. Montagu and P. Sorokin) when he says that "the most satisfying and most complete example of ego transcendence, and certainly the most healthy from the point of view of avoiding illness of the character, is the throwing of oneself into a

[1] *Becoming: Basic Considerations for a Psychology of Personality* (New Haven: Yale University Press, 1955), p. 94.

[2] I have tried to suggest grounds for belief in the goodness of God in "Can the Goodness of God Be Empirically Grounded," *Journal of Bible and Religion,* April 16, 1957. For a contrasting approach see John Hutchison, *Faith, Reason, and Existence* (New York: Oxford University Press, 1956).

healthy love relationship." [3] Professor Allport put this same thought crisply when he said: "Love received and love given comprise the best form of therapy." [4]

It is, then, to the very structure of human experience in its varied facets and accomplishments that we look for the confirmation of the Christian view of God and his purposes for men. The human attempt to give a coherent account of its own grasp and its own reach is the living root-system that supports Christian convictions. The "love of God" would be a meaningless phrase apart from the human experience of the kind of creative insecurity which permeates so many of our tiptoe experiences. [5]

Thus, far from saying that the Christian view. of the world and human destiny cannot be justified by analysis of human experience at its best, I suggest that no other outlook will lastingly hold man's loyalty. The Judeo-Christian view has gripped men because they found at its core convictions which spoke to their experience and inspired it to further growth. The Christian does not need to point to something "beyond human understanding," to justify his basic convictions and his way of life. His interpretation of life's meaning grows out of his attempt to make sense out of his many-sided experience of good and evil, of beauty and ugliness, of growth and decay, of order and disorder, of holiness and despair. He may not always be clear about the proper interpretation of his own intimate ventures, but his appeal, in the last

[3] A. H. Maslow, *Motivation and Personality* (New York: Harper & Brothers, 1954), p. 251.
[4] Gordon W. Allport, *Becoming* (New Haven, Conn.: Yale University Press, 1955), p. 33.
[5] The reader of Chapters 15, 16, 17 in my *Introduction to Philosophy of Religion* (New York: Prentice-Hall, Inc., 1951) will know that I am so impressed with evils for which man cannot be held responsible, that I think it important to reconsider some of the traditional theistic and Christian teaching, especially about God's omnipotence. But, however one resolves the problem created by the existence of non-disciplinary evil, the thesis I am expounding here is not endangered.

analysis, can be only to human experience fully appreciated, carefully organized, and courageously extended in his own faith for living.

What Does Belief in God Involve?

With this background, I want to clarify in this chapter a theme suggested in the first chapter, and then move on to show what happens to our thinking about God when we put the accent on creativity and love. Again, we cannot achieve thoroughness, but we can seek a fairly clear focus.

The world and man in religious perspective

Religious persons, we said in the first chapter, have had experiences which convince them that the world in which they live is more than a combination of matter, living plants, animals, and man. They hold that all these ultimately depend for their existence and continuation upon God. To "believe in God" can be a phrase so trite that I take recourse to an oversimplified diagram to bring out the contrast in the kind of world conceived by the nonbeliever and the believer in God.

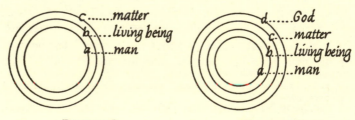

DIAGRAM I	DIAGRAM II
What constitutes the "world" for nonbelievers	What constitutes the "world" for believers

For the believer, Diagram I does not indicate the true state of affairs in the universe. Assuming that each circle represents a kind of being related to the two others, believers find that the most important circle is missing from the diagram. Thus, they would add another circle to express their conviction that we do not experience only atoms and stars, animals and plants, and our fellow men. We also can experience *a Presence in, through, and beyond these,* which is another Dimension, as it were, both of our lives and of the universe. The circles in Diagram I are merely used to bring out the fact that Deity is not the same as matter, life, and man, as we ordinarily experience and conceive these.

Nor are the words, "in, through, and beyond" to be taken as final. We shall not consider here whether God is to be conceived pantheistically as one with the world, or theistically as both beyond and creatively related to the world. (The latter is what I believe, and it also represents the major Judeo-Christian emphasis.) The fact of the matter is that most religious people do not concern themselves about the exact relation between the Presence they experience, and the rest of the world, and leave such questions to the metaphysical experts to consider. They believe that nature and man depend upon God in some mysterious way and turn their attention to the task of relating their living more effectively to this Being whom they worship. But when they come to define God's character they do not find it easy; and they frequently assign attributes to God which they would find incompatible anywhere else, but which they justify by appealing to the limitations of their own minds. We wish now to clarify one of the basic tensions in their thinking—or should we better say "our thinking"?

God as Almighty Power

Each of us finds God—and God finds us—in the midst of our total effort to discover and preserve "the things that matter most" in our lives. But what seems to matter most at one time seems to be relatively unimportant at another. As we have seen, the demand for security is a strong one. And it would be strange indeed if man did not think of God as the Provider and Protector.

As each of us looks into his own experience, he often finds himself thinking of God as Providence, that is, as the Being upon whom we depend for our own existence and that of all other beings. Even in our most unbelieving moments we find ourselves saying, do we not, "Yet, there must be something behind it all"? And then, thinking of what it must take to establish and to run this tremendous universe, we are indeed awed by the majesty of such Being. This God, we reflect, is the God of power; he is God Almighty; he can do "anything"—all the things we can imagine and all that we cannot. Yes, as we develop the conception of God that is implicit in our response to the grandeur of our cosmos and the majesty of its Creator and Controller, we can hear the stirring refrain from "The Messiah": "He is the King of Glory! He is the King of Glory!" and we rise to our feet in acclaim, in obedience to the emotion that wells up in us.

There is that in us which worships power—let there be no doubt about it. The person who can invent ingenious machines, the person who can build bridges, the person who can understand and control vast forces, this person arouses our respect, when he does not touch off our envy! Power, stupendous and tremendous, we fall before; we wish *we* had it and think of all the things we could do if only we could have it. Such are our real and felt limitations from day to day, that we think we would have everything, the real thing that matters most, if only we had all power—omnipotence. The cult of superman among us appeals to that side of our nature that seems to need, and stand in awe of, sheer power.

Nor am I thinking of the so-called "average man" when I call attention to that in us which worships power in all its mysterious capacities. Many of our most sensitive spirits [6]

[6] I am thinking of the great philosophical-theological tradition which stems from Neo-Platonic and Thomistic awareness that the ultimate Being can be better described in terms of what it is not, than by positive analogies. But I have in mind also thinkers like Paul Tillich and W. T. Stace who, whatever their differences, agree that attempts to conceptualize "unconditional" Being are bound to be misleading. It seems to me, as will be clear from the text, that although no concept is ever adequate to describe any dynamic being or event, the philosophical and theological task is to determine what concepts can be best trusted.

This may be the place to say a word to advanced readers which may clarify the underlying contrast between the perspective above and the thought of Professor Tillich. My presuppositions are those of a Personalistic Theism. On this view divine Being and finite persons are never one and never "participate in" or enjoy ontological identity, in Professor Tillich's more pantheistic sense. Professor Tillich, it seems to me, ultimately rejects the theistic doctrine of God's transcendence *and* immanence by moving in the direction of a part-whole relation between man and Unconditioned Being (his "God above God"). But this part-whole relationship seems to me to make of the doctrine of human freedom and individuality at critical points a matter of ecstatic words rather than concrete events. The only perspective which seems to me to protect experienced freedom, guilt, grace, worship, and goodness is one in which God, in accordance with his own loving nature and purpose, creates man, delegates to him limited freedom and power, and, in myriad ways, seeks to develop a creative fellowship of love between himself and men. For Tillich's part-whole relation between man and God a personalistic theist substitutes the freer relation of finite personal purposers to a creative cosmic Purposer, whose purpose involves their finite freedom. A personalistic analogy which, still inadequately, expresses the kind of part and whole involved is that of Composer-Conductor and co-creator musicians in an orchestra. The only identity ultimately possible between Creator and created-creator is one of growing co-operation in purpose and never of being.

Yet I know that Professor Tillich would insist that his view more adequately protects the initiative of both man and God. Better, then, to leave these issues for treatment elsewhere rather than in a book whose effort is to lay a foundation for other trips into the metaphysical depths and the theological stratosphere. But I fear that for me, courage *to become,* in different respects, on the part of both God and man, must be as ultimate as the "courage to be"; for to be, in ultimate terms, is to be a person, but to be a person is also to become.

have urged us to remember that God is a being so far removed from our own capacities and our own ways of con-
ceiving things, that nothing we can say, no concept, no figure
of speech can do justice to the greatness of God. At the very
best, we could try to describe God negatively—by saying that
he is not this and that he is not that; for no utterance of ours
could begin to grasp this Absolute Being.

If we keep this up, however, where would we end? If we
take in dead earnest such sayings as "His ways are not our
ways," that is, that nothing God does is in any sense like
anything that man does or has ever done, what *should* be
our *logical* conclusion?

Obviously, that we know nothing about Him—not even
that we are dependent on him. For if nothing we can think
can begin to grasp what his nature is like, we must, in all
strictness, say that even our ideas of dependence-independ-
ence do not apply to him. If, for example, God's black can
be our white, if our wisdom can be sheer foolishness to him,
we have no reason to trust any judgment about him.

Similarly, try to conceive of Power as some all-out kind
of being that simply has no power-limitation, and what do
we discover? We soon are forced either to speak nonsense,
or to reconsider what "omnipotence" can mean if it is to
make sense. We begin to realize, for example, that when we
think of omnipotence—of all the power there is or can be—
we are forced to think of it as Power to do something or
other, and not "everything" at once. It is only when we
neglect this fact that we ask whether God could make a
mountain without a valley, and even, whether he could kill
himself and come to life again! In a word, whenever we try
to think of Power as sheer power, or power in the abstract,
as power that "can do anything," we find that we have gone
from the *feeling* of awe, that accompanies some concrete,
moving experience of ours, to sheer nonsense and abraca-
dabra.

What is perfect power?

I am pressing this point because I believe that under the sway of the so-called "perfection of power" we have seriously confused our thinking about God. We may have begun by saying that God's capacities far outreach our own limitations, but then we have gone on to say that we simply could not comprehend his nature in any way. In so doing we have also confused our thinking about the standard by which to judge human goodness. We have said, for example, that any human act is right and good just because God ordains it.

But if the Omnipotent Power we worship were simply the All-powerful Being in the world, would we really worship him, or continue to do so? If such a Being, for example, should, like Herod, ordain that all children in the world be slain, giving no reason for this, except that he willed it, would we, nay, *should* we, worship him? I can imagine that we might in fear bow our heads, but I cannot imagine that we would continue to worship such a Being.

The reader may, at this point, wonder whether I am simply beating the air with some refined, idle point I have in mind. I am, unfortunately, raising a matter which we have allowed to lie idle too long while human beings lost their way. I have seen too many young people seriously affected by this emphasis on doing the will of God just because it is the will of the most powerful Being in the world. Two college students recently said that they could understand fearing God but not loving him. As one put it, "Ever since I can remember, my parents have impressed on me the 'fear of the Lord,' and in my church I have been told that whatever God willed, regardless of the consequences—this was to be done, or—." What else, I ask, can we expect from emphasis on the conception of God as a "jealous God," a Being who keeps strict accounts of who did and who did not obey his edict! In a word, a God who is considered God simply because he is the Ultimate or the most powerful Being conceivable may arouse our anxieties, but we in fact do not, and cannot, worship such a cosmic "bogey man."

Actually, as we reflect upon the matter, we discover that though we do stand in awe of power, we never worship it simply because it is power (or creativity). We worship power only when it attempts and produces certain goods. It is not the quantity of total power that we worship; it is the qualities or values which total power produces. When total power produces us as human beings, when we find ourselves in a physical world to which we are conformed enough to make our survival possible, when we find that we can learn from the laws of Nature, from our own nature, yes, when we appreciate the way in which things depend upon each other and support each other, then we begin to appreciate the overarching *wisdom* of that power. Wisdom is that quality we attribute to Power when its activities in an enterprise are co-ordinated with each other in such a way as to avoid conflict between the parts in the light of the purpose.

For example, if we hired a carpenter to crate a chair for us, we should hardly consider him wise if he built the crate so strongly that it became quite troublesome to lift, or if he built it so that it could not fit through the doorway of the room it was in. What is wise, then, depends on the purpose to be achieved. Wisdom has to do with the over-all conception, and with the fittingness, of the parts to work together with the purpose of the whole. We thus come back to the same conclusion: It is not naked Power without wisdom that we worship. It is Power that is wise as judged by the purpose to which it is devoted, and by the way in which the goal is reached. And here we must ask: What would be the wisest purpose for which power could be dedicated?

What power can we worship?

We are now at another critical point in our thinking, for it is very tempting at this point to say: How can we tell? Are we not being presumptuous to suppose that we can answer a question like this? Thus, that ancient roadblock to sustained reflection, *skepticism in the cloak of humility,* confronts us again.

To be sure, anyone who has struggled with philosophical and theological problems frequently comes to the point of self-questioning where he asks: How do I know I am correct, or that I can ever be correct? How can I suppose that the schemes I think up can begin to tell me what reality is like? And well he may! Such self-searching and self-doubt can keep him cautious and discourage boasting. But caution and humility are good only when they keep one working away at his problem, doing the best he can. They ought never to be an excuse for quitting. After all, if one says: "I cannot possibly know," he is saying: "I know that the world is such that I cannot know." This is his judgment also!

No, he must start, again, where he is; and we must do the same. We cannot have it both ways. We cannot think "there's no use thinking" and accept this conclusion of thinking! We must think, and we must be consistent and persistent in thinking. But even this is not enough. We must think consistently and persistently about every kind of human experience and fact. We must develop theories which help us to see the relations between our experiences, between all the facts we have accumulated, and the values we have appreciated. Careful thinking takes every kind of experience and knowledge into account, and realizes that our conclusions must ever be revised by growth in experience and knowledge.

Fortunately, in asking ourselves what the wisest purpose may be to which power could be dedicated, we do not start from scratch. We have much knowledge and we have a great deal of experience which we cannot overlook. And we must give the best answer we can in the light of that knowledge and experience. Each of us must give his answer, for each of us also has power to devote to some aim. To what can power be most wisely given?

I have already suggested my own answer to this question. It seems to me that power is most wisely used when it develops means to help free, conscious persons to help themselves grow. Power used to enslave—yes, even a benevolent despotism in which the enslaved persons enjoy freedom from pain, from insecurity, from making mistakes—is despicable power, even if it is not "violent," for it does not allow human beings the freedom to choose for themselves within limits. It increases and puts the control of power all in one agent, when it should be so distributed that others also could enjoy freedom-in-power and power-in-freedom—and the resultant creative insecurity! If power is good in one agency, if power to create is good at one source, why is it not good at as many points as possible?

But, what does such power-in-freedom involve in terms of human experience? Once more I am driven back to an earlier conclusion. And once more I can only use the highest quality of power that I know in human experience—the power of creative love, the power devoted to encouraging the creativity-in-love of persons—as the basis for my estimate of what an infinite Power could wisely sustain. This is the best I know, the devotion of ability or power to the development of conscious, free, reflective control of ability in oneself and in others, so that a free co-operation in the growth of tensively-balanced personalities results. This kind of power, be it noted, endangers power for the sake of power, for it opposes arbitrary power. But it promotes the growth of power in all beings for the sake of fellowship-in-power.

And this is the zenith of love—mutual appreciation and mutual concern for the growth in freedom.

It is hardly necessary to reformulate the answer to the question: How would the wisest Being use his Power? The Wisest of agents would use the best methods possible to support, challenge, and encourage persons who know the meaning of choice to use that capacity creatively. The most Powerful of beings would be wisest when he used that power to produce other self-conscious agents who would share the quality of power exemplified by his own creativity-in-power.

And this, I take it, is essentially the view of God central in Christian thinking and worship. The Power of God is the Power of love. The Love of God is his will to do all he can to encourage the development of other free centers and sources of love. Over and over again we have heard it said that the Christian God is the God of love, the God who cares for persons as individuals, the God who has given and gives of himself for their salvation as persons. And this is the view which I find most consistent with the best we know about human life and experience.

The Meaning of God's Perfection

The God who needs nothing beyond himself

But great Christian thinkers, as well as the rest of us, have sometimes given this view of God more lip service than true centrality. This is understandable for, as I have suggested, there is something in us that responds to sheer power. And the Christian tradition, in any case, has been swift to rise to the defense of God's majesty and power, whenever anyone has seemed to prune it in any way. The majority of Christian theologians could not, for example, think of God as being limited by some entity outside himself, like matter, to which he would have to conform in any way in his own efforts to use it. And there were understandable reasons for this concern. An all-powerful God could not brook eternal opposition to his will and still be God all-powerful.

In this mood, therefore, stress is laid on the omnipotence of a cosmic Potentate, and in this mood we respond to the Psalmist's strains: "The earth is the Lord's and the fullness thereof; the world, and they that dwell therein. For he hath founded it upon the seas, and established it upon the floods." [7] And, indeed, who can but be impressed by the grandeur of the cosmos? Who does not have a "creature feeling" in the presence of the Maker and Creator of all the galaxies? Here is one Being, we say, who depends on nothing else for his existence, and upon whom all existent things depend for their being. Here is one Being, then, who is safe against all the inroads of time and decay. To his powers there is no end, and infinite he is, that is, complete in every way imaginable, and not in want of anything.

Out of this trend of feeling and of thought there arises a concept of a Perfect Being whose perfection consists in the fact that in him there is nothing missing, and every attribute is complete. Thus, the "I am that I am" who spoke to Moses is a Being whose nature as self-sufficient Being could involve nothing short of full, completed being, that is, no imperfection. With this kind of perfect Being in mind, we go on to say (as great thinkers like Augustine and Aquinas as well as many of our contemporaries say) that God cannot change, no, not even by a jot and tittle. Indeed, if he has all that is worth having, to what can he change?

I would not have the reader suppose that the most refined reasoning has not been advanced by philosophers and theologians in favor of this view of perfection, or that this question can be dispensed with as easily as I may seem to do. But I am concerned that as we study these arguments we keep in mind also what is required by consistency among our conceptions. "What consistency has been violated?" I

[7] Psalm 24:1, 2, King James Version.

am asked. We cannot see it clearly until we take one more step in the reasoning we were just outlining.

It was said, and by Christian thinkers also, that since God is perfect, since he has no imperfections in his nature, then surely he cannot suffer. God is impassive; no distress can be a part of his experience. He must be above all suffering. But this means that God does not really share in suffering. This "impassivity" does not mean simply that God, like a skilled surgeon, must not allow his operation to be affected by the painful cries of his patient. It means also that, he, a perfect, complete God, cannot ever be in want; and he therefore cannot in his experience undergo the imperfection involved in suffering.

The inconsistency should now be clear, for the God of perfection (when power and completeness is emphasized) is not the God of perfection (when love for creativity in other persons is emphasized). The God of love is the God who suffers. He is the God in whom rejoicing supplants sadness when the prodigal son has returned home. The God of perfect power who has all, who does not need anything, whose nature is subject to no change, is clearly contradicted by the God who loves man and gives himself and suffers that man may be free and come of himself back to the Father. The Christian, I contend, cannot worship both Gods. He cannot, consistently, worship both the completeness of power and the completeness of love, even though there is that in his nature which is fascinated by both, psychologically.

Can love ever mean absolute power?

What is really at stake, of course, is the underlying issue which we have been discussing in the last two chapters. What do we really mean by a perfect Being? Shall we insist on one who changes in no respect? If so, we must give up the notion of a creative being, for a creative being is a being who in some sense adds to what already is. Shall we insist on one who is perfect, safe, beyond the reach of insecurity? If so, we must give up productive love, for can the God who is safe and serene against all change, the God who is never insecure in any respect, can that God know the kind of insecurity which is the essence of forgiving love? Perhaps at this point we had better press the question: Must love be inconsistent with absolute power? And again we are driven back to clarifying the meaning we are to give to "love" and "power."

If "love" means the willingness to control oneself in such a way as to help other free persons to develop their character and personality (up to a certain point, at least) according to their own convictions, then, as we have seen, a real risk to the development of equanimity is inevitable. Freedom is a value fraught with danger and forever surrounded by some insecurity and uncertainty. When human beings were endowed by God with freedom, they were blessed by the experience of creativity within the limits of their abilities. But now the way was open to every kind of uncertainty, danger, and torture which their abilities allowed. For human beings, freedom abused or used with inadequate insight spells suffering; and the history of freedom, unenlightened or abused, is the history of human agony and woe.

Can it be otherwise for God? Is he not disturbed when his children to whom he has delegated limited freedom become frustrated? (I always mean freedom within limits, therefore I shall not repeat the word "limited.") There are at least two ways in which God is affected.

First, if we are to hold that God's wisdom includes purposes for all human beings, then, if human beings are free, God must wait for them to make the decisions he would have them make. Furthermore, he must "make do" and improvise in the light of the decisions they make. Even to put a thought like this so boldly into words seems blasphemous to many! Imagine a Being like God held up in his plans by frail and puny creatures like us! Yet, let us face it. Is not God waiting upon human effort to see to it that so many starving persons be fed, that the unclothed be clothed, that the ill be tended, that the ignorant be better educated, that the dispossessed share in the goods of this world, that the discouraged find sympathy and trust, that the lonely be comforted? And must God not wait, in our individual lives, for us to make the decisions that will lead to our growth? Does he not have purposes for our lives with which we fail to co-operate, thus forcing him to give up the achievement of some values which could have been realized had we willed our level best?

Second, God is forced not only to wait and to improvise, but, if he cares, as we must assume he does, there is real disappointment and heartache in his life. The God who would draw us, as Jesus said of Jerusalem, under his wings as a hen draws her chicks, must weep, even as Jesus wept when he contemplated the suffering which his people were inflicting upon each other simply because they would not trust and love and share with each other, or turn with penitent hearts to the God of their fathers. Human freedom is the cross which God imposed upon himself, knowing that this cross would involve misunderstanding, contempt, disbelief, and disloyalty. If to give us freedom is to love us, if to give man freedom is to share the responsibility for creativity, then to give us freedom is to invite suffering. The Christian, of all religious persons, should be the last person to cloud or minimize this fact, for when once understood and appreciated, it becomes the power unto righteousness, as we have already seen.

But such is the hold of the image of "perfect power" that thought has been given to preserve God's power, wisdom, and serenity against the inroads of human freedom. In a word, we have wanted God to love us but without paying any real price for it. I fear that I am one of those people that simply cannot see how this can be done. It has even been said that God's wisdom and power are so great that he would know how to gain his ends regardless of what man did, that man would not be allowed to slow down or alter God's purposes.

Does God foreknow all?

Two considerations ought to render such a contention more than questionable. First, we are responsible for the clearest thinking we can do on this matter. Until we can show how the future of a free person can be predicted in every detail, we should go slowly about making such statements. I am not questioning for a moment that God knows all there is to be known, or that nothing happens that is beyond God's knowledge at the time that it happens. Nor am I questioning that wherever predictions can be made upon the basis of the past, God will know what to predict. And I would insist that God knows all the possibilities that could possibly be known at any one time in the world-process, so that he can know "infinitely" more about the future than we know. In other words, once a given human being makes a move on the cosmic checkerboard (to improvise one of William James' illustrations), God knows all the possibilities now open to him.

But two things seem clear to me. God cannot know the exact detail of a free volition. God knows the possibilities open to the agent and he knows the structure of the situation confronted, and the capacities of the agent. But if he already knows what the agent will do in every case, there is no point to talking about the free will of the agent; for, again, to be free does not mean that one can do anything. But it does mean that in some areas at any rate the individual, and the individual alone, decides which, of at least two alternatives open to him, he will take. If anybody else already knows that he will take a given alternative, then the alternative is not really an alternative, but a path which he had to take given his present structure and the situation. I am not saying that human beings are always correct when they think they are free, but I am saying that if they are ever free, as they seem quite frequently to be, then the *exact detail,* the specific choice, cannot be predicted and still be a choice!

If this is the general situation, then we can also say that God can know the possibilities open to groups of men and of nations once a given course has been decided upon. But as long as he respects the freedom of human beings, he must wait until they make their decisions before he knows what new areas of possibility they thus open to themselves because of this choice. One who knows the "lay of the land" will know where a motorist who takes one of several forks in the road will be. But, in so far as the motorist is free to make the choice, the observer will not know what choice the motorist will make before the motorist himself does.

A second consideration should sober the contention that God will not allow his purposes for mankind to be retarded by man. If God were to have his way "regardless," we would be forced to suppose that God is more concerned about "man" or "mankind" than men! Perhaps we need to take firmer hold on the fact that, after all is said and done, God does not love "man"; he loves men, men one by one, men with unique capacities and possibilities of choice. In the last analysis, God's battle is for every life and in every life. Each person chooses, and his choices influence the larger choice of the corporate groups. But it is not the corporate group alone that wins or fails, for, whatever the group does, the individual must win or lose the battle for righteousness of will in his own life. This must not be taken to mean that God cares only for the individual; nay, through the choices of one individual the choices of another are affected. The drunken driving of a man who has chosen to drink affects and limits the choices of those who share the road with him. But, and this is the point, God works for creative insecurity in every life, in the constant individual battle that the better prevail over the worse. If God is to insist that his ends be gained no matter what individuals and groups do, he will have to step in and control the action of individuals about to make any decisions prejudicial to his end—and this is to negate their freedom.

What is God's plan?

We would not make this kind of mistake, however, if, when we thought of "God's plans," we remembered that as long as freedom for creativity is central to God's plan, then God's plan *is* being realized. In other words, it *is God's plan being carried out,* when he is forced to delay, improvise, and even give up some possible goods by the fact that man freely chooses other motives He does not approve. On this view, God is not a cosmic Potentate who gives and negates freedom only in so far as his subjects fit into preconceived plans. God is a creative Father whose plans are constantly changing in the light of his central aim, of allowing his children to be co-creative in the process of developing themselves and their fellow men. *The power of God is the power of creative love.* Power there is, but it is power dedicated constantly to maintaining the best conditions possible, consistent with the freedom of men. God is forced, by his very love for us, to let us go even when he would not; he is forced to allow us to suffer and to hurt each other. But he does not turn back, and he never gives us up, co-operating gladly rather than sadly, with every decision we make which is productively creative.

There is one practical consequence from this discussion. We cannot allow ourselves the specious comfort, for example, of those who say: "God will not allow man to destroy himself by the abuse of nuclear energy." Nations have come and gone, and we may have come to the point of critical decision. The wages of sin are death, and God and man will both suffer if the wrong choice is made. But God will go on, working as creatively as possible with what we leave! There is a judgment of God in history and upon history; but it is a judgment that represents God's love and God's sacrifice as well as man's failure to live up to the requirements of love.

The God We Worship: Redemptive Sufferer

We no sooner said that there is that in us which worships power than we began to wonder whether man would ever really worship naked power. We suspected that the awe man feels in its presence is fear rather than respect or reverence. And we wondered, further, whether man has not worshiped power only when he has unconsciously *assumed* that the power was being used wisely and would always be used for good ends. That power grips us I do not doubt, but that we ever really think of power except as power to accomplish certain desired ends is questionable. Power that overcomes and threatens may bring us to our knees quivering with fear, pleading for mercy, supplicating that we be spared. In this situation we cry from our weakness, from the full realization that our lives depend upon Something Beyond which can arbitrarily destroy us if it will. But our very pleading presupposes that we at least hope that it will not be sheer power, indifferent to pain and to what we hold dear. And, as we think out what power we admire we find that it is power that is wise in the achievement of its ends.

What is it, then, that we do *worship?* When do we find ourselves falling to our knees in adoration, inspired and drawn by a fascination that grips the core of our being—a fascination that makes us feel that this is what matters most, that there can be no better engagement of our energies than in devotion to this Reality? Here I suggest once more that we proceed from the best that we know in our human experience, being rigorously honest with ourselves, and not giving the "conventional" responses which we might be tempted to give. 1 may be wrong in what I am about to say, but at least it represents this stage of my development, and so I shall not hesitate to share it with my readers.

The best in human experience

I find myself adoring the quality which I have called forgiving love. When I see a human being who gives of his energy and thought for the sake of another's creative growth, when I see a love through which respect for the freedom of other persons grows, I *nearly* reach the climax of admiration, reverence, and adoration. But I go "all out" and find a new depth in my response when I note that even though the person who is loved returns evil for love, the person who loves him still finds patience, understanding, and constant concern that condemns the sin, but forgives the sinner. Forgiving love, love committed to the growth of the other *no matter what,* love that maintains the conditions for fellowship no matter what the beloved does—this is the kind of power I find almost impossible to understand. Did I not witness it at least in part in many human actions, in the many heroic acts of renunciation which give life dignity, I would not understand it at all.

We are back, the reader will see, to the value of values, to the pearl of great price, the creativity of forgiving love. I know nothing better in human affairs. I can only marvel at the depth and breadth of compassion in a man of the dimensions of Albert Schweitzer. Schweitzer gives us a glimpse into the quality of his life when he says:

Only at quite rare moments have I felt really glad to be alive. I could not but feel with a sympathy full of regret all the pain that I saw around me, not only that of men but that of the whole creation. From this community of suffering I have never tried to withdraw myself. It seemed to me a matter of course that we should all take our share of the burden of pain which lies upon the world.[8]

And when I see a Gandhi both feel for his people and do his utmost to share in their suffering; when I see him yearning to share their burdens and yet unwilling to budge in his dedication to their good even when they scorn him, then, indeed, my admiration comes close to adoration.

And if I speak of almost adoring that rare quality of compassion and creative love as it shines forth in a Gandhi and a Schweitzer, what shall I say of him whose Sermon on the Mount is nonsense unless his religion means creative insecurity? Yet behind and in the Sermon, giving it a fire which burns in bone and muscle, and a light which glows when words no longer suffice, is the life whose essential stature must surely outrun the portrayal in the Gospels. May I say here that any doctrine about Jesus as "the Christ," the son of God, would leave me cold unless the Jesus I meet in the Gospels, and the God to whom he prayed, brought me to my knees on a new peak of experience.

Even were I capable, this would hardly be the place to go into detail on matters of biblical criticism involving the portrayal of Jesus. But unless my students (let me be professional and restrictive) could critically find in the man who walked in Galilee, living "by every word that proceedeth from the mouth of God," a person who could bring them to their highest point of moral and religious sensitivity, any doctrine of the Christ as the Son of God, would become a ludicrous intellectual chore. No, it is the Jesus who saw in each person the child of God, who lived conscientiously, but humbly and compassionately, among his fellow men, who accepted at their hands unearned ingratitude, hatred, and even contemptuous mocking and yet forgave them; it is the Jesus

[8] Albert Schweitzer, *Out of My Life and Thought*, tr. by C. T. Campion (New York: Henry Holt and Company, Inc., 1932). Used by permission of the publishers.

who, as Gethsemane showed, grew in his ennobling, tragic sense of what it means to be the loving Father of men, and then died without self-pity for their sakes—it is this Jesus who can give me some sense of what it would mean for God to walk among men. And no theory of the universe I may spin can disregard the fact that this kind of forgiving love became evident in Jesus and transformed the lives of millions and their history.

The best in the cosmos

If I can feel this way about creative love as it is seen "in the flesh," how do I feel when I contemplate the way in which the cosmic Person uses his power? All words then fail to express the quality of reverence, the unique feeling of awe, the sense of the nothingness of my own accomplishments, the strangling gratitude and new humility, and that other quality, *blessedness,* which adds its own unique quality to these others.

To be less personal, when a man contemplates the fact that the Maker of the cosmos saw fit to create finite human persons, endow them with a freedom which they could abuse, sustain them in that freedom even when they reject his will for themselves and for others, when, I say, a man allows this situation really to filter through his consciousness, he is gripped by a new sense of life's possibility. He must contemplate a God who does not withdraw his support from sinful, heedless, contemptuous men as they appropriate the world to their purposes. This God goes on maintaining the order of Nature which they now use as if they owned it. He responds in his own being to all the suffering in the world, necessary and unnecessary, but he never gives up, in every moral effort open to him, the attempt to help and redeem men.

The words "sinful" and "redeem" have just been used. Some of my readers will wonder how "sin" is different from maladjustment, and why Christians fuss so much about "redemption" and "forgiveness." In the first chapter I maintained that a mature religion is itself a creative attempt to understand and fulfill human needs. In most of the remainder of this book I have tried to indicate how penetrating and pervasive is the need to be loved and to love creatively. And I have just been insisting that the love which is most creative is the love which is forgiving. Indeed, my basic reason for believing that the Christian perspective in religion is the truest one is that, as I see it, the Christian can never use the word "love" sentimentally, but must rather spell LOVE in practice as FORGIVENESS. But we cannot appreciate the emphasis on forgiveness unless we realize the kind of state the Christian describes as sin. Let me pause, then, to give an analogy which may illustrate the situation in which "the state of sin" and "the need for forgiveness" arises.

Suppose a man is wedded to a wife who loves him, trusts him, and has expressed her love for him in myriad ways. Nevertheless, of his own free will he becomes unfaithful to her. After he has broken the bond of faith—notice, *he* has broken it—how does he feel? He feels unworthy of her love; he feels alienated and estranged; he feels that a chasm exists between him and his beloved. This is analogous to the state of sin. Sin is the severing of the tie of love, the turning of one's back on the one who has trusted him. What does a husband who sins against his wife experience? He feels guilty! He may repent! He may buy candy and flowers! He may offer to sacrifice this and that! But will this alone do? No! The only thing that will close the gap is her reaching out toward him and saying: "I cannot approve, but I can try to forget. I forgive you."

And if she forgives him, what will she do? She will go on living with him, not in condescending "tolerance," but with understanding and sympathy. She does not draw away from him in smug purity, but she joins him in rebuilding their relationship of love. Thus, his sin is indeed washed away; he feels a new man, redeemed. But his redemption began with her forgiveness, and his repentance with conviction that she still loved him, despite his sin.

This analogy may be suggestive for the relation of man to God and the meaning of sin, as the Christian sees it. The love of a Creator-Person, we have seen, is central to Christian thought. God created man not as a puppet, but free. He put at his disposal a Garden of Eden, that is, a world of order in which man could fulfill many of his needs. God created man with limited freedom of will because he wanted man to be a co-creator, not just another thing. Let an Adam appreciate this fact. Let him feel the goodness of a God who entrusted him with his world and with his fellow men. Let him realize that the world is not his, no part of it; that his neighbor is not a tool to be used and then dropped as if he were a thing. But then, just because he is free, just because he would be creative, let him be tempted to treat himself as the Creator, and treat the world and his fellow men as if they were made only for his private satisfaction. Let him, like Cain, deny that he is his brother's keeper. In short, let man treat God as if God were his servant, and his fellow men his pawns! What happens to him—whatever happens to those he has hurt?

Deep in him he feels his nakedness! He flees and hides himself; he may even try to blame God—"the woman thou gavest me"—and his fellow men for his own faults! But he knows that he has abused his freedom! And he feels estranged, alienated, chained to his sin. "Woe is me, for I am undone!" In this state of sin, separated from the Holy One, what can he do? Can he by himself right all the wrong? Can he by sacrifice balance the scales? Can anything he does by himself, unilaterally, wipe the slate clean?

In this situation the Christian, following some paths already laid down in the Old Testament, felt that ultimately the situation could be righted only by an act on God's part.

Man alone had made the breach, but he could not heal it alone. Only a Father who loved him enough could be the scapegoat, take the burden of man's sin upon himself, and thus save man. Though his sins were as scarlet, he could be as white as snow only if God himself stepped mercifully into his life and said: Rise, and sin no more!

I would stress once more that the essential Christian belief here is in God's forgiving love, the love which does not deal with a man according to justice or even equality—the love which is willing to suffer through man's sin and suffer for man's sin in order to win man back into the renewing fellowship. It is true that Jews, Christians, and Moslems, have disagreed about the scheme of redemption from sin. Nevertheless, schemes of redemption presuppose the loving forgiveness of God.

What the proper scheme is, I shall not even attempt to consider here; Christian churches have disagreed as to how God saves men. The dominant tradition has been that only the death and resurrection of Jesus, the son of God, "very God of very God," could wash away man's sin and give man confidence in God's love. There are careful analyses of the "atonement" (at-one-ment) that any fully intelligent Christian must evaluate; by not mentioning them here I do not mean to suggest that these doctrines are unimportant. But I would focus attention on the essential theme which must not be lost from sight, the quality of the love of God, a Love that suffers when human beings sin, yet a Love which forgives and takes home the prodigal son who has wasted his own and his father's substance.

To return to our main theme: the Love which we can worship is the love God has for men, by which men are drawn together as persons and as God's children. It is a love unto forgiveness. It springs from the realization that men who are free to be co-creators may also be sinners and need to be brought back to a relation of trust and confidence.

When a man feels he is so loved he is freer to see his fellow man in a new light. He begins to catch the new vision of what life can mean for him as a member of the Kingdom ruled by dedication to God's love for all. We have already seen that nothing in the life of an erring child can more surely make him want to be better than the realization that those upon whom he depends care for him so much that they are anxious to join him in rebuilding goodness into his life. So the children of God, once they realize that they are his children, find themselves anxious to be forgiven, and to co-operate with God and their fellow men in the process of cleansing their lives of evil and committing themselves to the greatest good open to them.

When forgiveness redeems

Does this mean that their past sin is no more? Yes, if it means that it will not be charged against them by God, either now or in the future. For God or for man, to forgive completely is to forget. That is, it is to add no penalty, that can possibly be avoided, to the deed already done. But it cannot mean that the evil done in one's life and in the life of others is undone. That suffering, that evil, has made its mark upon man and God, and the sinner and those sinned against must endure it. But when a past sin is seen in the light of a greater present effort the sadness, which reflection upon it brings, becomes a background and incentive for nobler living. Both man and God "wash" sin away not by some mechanical absolution which dissolves the past, but by beginning again with confidence, and with new wisdom and trust. A man may fail again; however, if he does, he fails in a new context which does not erase the failure, but makes it worth risking.

Something like this, I suggest, is what happens to men when they become aware of the venture in which their Soulmaker is engaged. And they combine in their own venture a sense of abandon which looks beyond the petty securities of life, for now men do not feel self-pity because they suffer. They are overcome by compassion with those who suffer, and they are inspired whenever that suffering is creative. The whole of life is different, for the great fear is not of failure, but of needless, useless failure; the horror is of the little successes which obscure the real issues of life. Their problem is not whether they fail, but in what, for what purpose they fail. Their problem is not whether they suffer, but what their suffering creates. And these men earn that inner peace, "not as the world giveth," namely, *the blessedness* which comes into human life when there is self-control for the sake of creativity.

The God Who Bears the Cross

Some who read this book may mark the fact that I have not tried to prove a point by reference to Jesus. But it must now be clear that much of what I have tried to say (and much more I do not know how to say) I have learned from my inadequate efforts to understand the life of Jesus and to be guided by his vision. I am sure that there are those who will say, with justification, as they read some of what I have said, that I have much to learn and have even missed the profoundest part. Be that as it may. But as I rethink much that I have read and learned, I find myself returning again and again to something like the preceding reflections as the core of Jesus' own living and teaching. In so far as I have tried to feel and understand the Presence, it seems most adequately reflected in the vision that motivated the Carpenter of Nazareth, the vision that transformed his life as it claimed his complete being. He saw that a God of love must suffer without ever making suffering an end in itself. He saw that love must forever center not on the deed alone, but on the spirit of concern in which the deed is done.

But even beyond "the deed" and "the spirit of the deed," there is that ideal, that goal, that renewing experience, which is at once the growing edge of every creative human striving, and the fruition of every inventive urge. Is there a more originative and more pregnant human experience than that blessedness which I shall here call the *fellowship of the compassionate*? Again I see this in the Jesus of the Gospels. The compassionateness of Jesus goes beyond sentimental tenderness; it is permeated by patient dedication to the struggle each person undergoes as he tries to allow the mustard seed of the spirit of Heaven to grow within him. It knows not the smugness and complacency of the Publican, for it is too fully concerned with the plight of a society in which there is suffering and sin. As Jesus placed each of his disciples within the frame of God's compassionate love, he gave himself to their growth. An adulterous woman, condemned by adulterous minds, found in Jesus not condescending pity, but concern. A scorned Zaccheus became the host of him who understood the conflict in his life. In what situation did Jesus lose that sense of fellowship with God which can transform every human being and enable him, even in the midst of insecurity and suffering, to feel blessed?

The fellowship with God which Jesus sought to share with others was one which was inspired by a quality beyond "obedience," by a sharing in the common goal of creative growth. Thus, God's first question to every man is not: Are you being faithful and obedient to me? His first question, so to put it, is this: Are you loyal to the best in you, and in your fellow man? Not that the question of obedience is less than paramount. But we cannot answer the question, What does obedience to God, what does "making God central" in one's life, mean, without going back to what it is that God does for man.

And the great answer given by the followers of Jesus is

this: God created creative men for fellowship, and God, through his work in nature, through the varied promptings of his spirit, does all in his power to inspire and help men to develop the fellowship of creative love. To be obedient to God, to be loyal to God, is to share co-operatively in what he is seeking to do for us and for our neighbors. It is to share in the most creative venture there is, the nurture and sustenance of persons.

All this may seem too moralistic, but it will seem so only to those who think of morality as a calculating "doing of good," instead of the level of living I have in mind. All be-havior that is really good begins as a man "thinketh in his heart," and it is always to be judged by the quality of fellow-ship it produces and inspires among men. We cannot ap-proach the throne of God's gracious care for us with anger toward our fellow men in our hearts. We can ask for forgive-ness of our sins "as we forgive those who sin against us." It is the heightened awareness of the fact that in God's world all human beings are to feel God's creative concern for them-selves and for each other—this is the fulcrum of Jesus' life, and of those who follow him. The truly prodigal son of God, as Jesus saw, is not so much he who sins, repents, and turns to his Father, but he who has not been saddened, as the Father has been, by the wandering son, and who cannot re-joice at the return of the sinner.

In a word, the crucial emphasis in what seems to me to be the way of Jesus is on a quality of fellowship between man-and-God and man-through-God-to-man. This fellowship is the only fellowship which is willing to sacrifice every con-sideration of mere security for growth. It is the fellowship-of-the-forgivers. It is the fellowship of the sinners who realize that their sin, above all, is to betray the fellowship of trust. It is the fellowship of those who have a constant sense of a life their spirits need. It is the fellowship of those who know that they can bear injustice without giving way to it because they are sustained by an unfaltering sense that only love "never faileth."

Such persons are a peculiar phenomenon among men. They are not "happy," for they cannot forget the cries of the innocent who have been needlessly hurt. They do not have "peace of mind" because they know that there can be no peace of mind when one has a gnawing sense of a fuller concern. But, strangely, theirs is a kind of serenity which never hides from what still needs to be done, and never flees from the discouraging or the painful. They have a kind of strength of mind, a maturity of spirit, which makes them forever grateful for every good, and forever yearning for the better. They are adventurous minds which are not restless and nervous.

Again, I know no other way of describing the quality of such lives than by using the word by which Jesus, in the Sermon on the Mount, described the consequences of living as a member of God's family. Jesus promised men blessedness. The blessed are not "happy" and they do not have peace of mind, for they will know sorrow and mourning as they try to live in creative insecurity with others and with God. They will know persecution "falsely, for my sake," but they will still be able to pray for their enemies. The person who lives in this spirit will know that ineffable quality of creative insecurity which constitutes blessedness. And he will know it because religion to him will always be a sharing in the Cross which binds the universe and man together in creative love.

Selected Bibliography

The following books, expressing different perspectives, are selected as helpful and challenging to the beginner. Despite their differences, they say much which a person trying to think his way into religion and moral life needs to consider.

Allport, Gordon W., *The Individual and His Religion* (New York: The Macmillan Company, 1950).

————, *Becoming. Basic Considerations for a Psychology of Personality* (New Haven, Conn.: Yale University Press, 1955).

Brightman, Edgar Sheffield, *The Finding of God* (New York: Abingdon Press, 1931).

————, *The Problem of God* (New York: Abingdon Press, 1930).

DeWolf, L. Harold, *A Theology of the Living Church* (New York: Harper & Brothers, 1953).

Ferré, Nels F. S., *Faith and Reason* (New York: Harper & Brothers, 1946).

Fromm, Erich, *Man for Himself* (New York: Rinehart & Company, Inc., 1947).

————, *The Art of Loving* (New York: Rinehart & Company, Inc., 1956).

Garnett, Arthur C., *Religion and the Moral Life* (New York: Ronald Press, 1955).

Harkness, Georgia E., *Foundations of Christian Knowledge* (New York: Abingdon Press, 1955).

————, *Christian Ethics* (New York: Abingdon Press, 1957).

Hazelton, Roger, *On Proving God* (New York: Harper & Brothers, 1952).

127

Hutchison, John, *Faith, Reason and Existence* (New York: Oxford University Press, 1956).

Johnson, Paul E., *Religion and Personality* (New York: Abingdon Press, 1957).

Maslow, A. H., *Motivation and Personality* (New York: Harper & Brothers, 1954).

Niebuhr, Reinhold, *An Interpretation of Christian Ethics* (New York: Harper & Brothers, 1935).

Pittenger, W. Norman, *Rethinking the Christian Message* (Greenwich, Conn.: Seabury Press, 1956).

Stace, W. T., *Time and Eternity* (Princeton, N. J.: Princeton University Press, 1952).

Tillich, Paul, *The Courage to Be* (New Haven, Conn.: Yale University Press, 1952).

———, *Dynamics of Faith* (New York: Harper & Brothers, 1957).

Ulich, Robert, *The Human Career* (New York: Harper & Brothers, 1955).